Natural Health
For Your Bird

Bernard Dorenkamp

Natural Health Care For Your

Bird

**Quick Self-Help Using
Homeopathy and Bach Flowers**

Translation from the German by
Elizabeth D. Crawford
Drawings by György Jankovics

Contents

What You Should Know About Your Bird

Treating Illnesses Yourself

Techniques for the Bird Owner

Appendix

Treating Illnesses Yourself

What You Should Know About Your Bird

Birds fascinate and charm us with their pretty colors, their beautiful voices, their unrestrained temperaments, and their ability to rise into the air, apparently weightless. Taking them into our homes is an attempt to obtain a bit of their unfettered ease of existence.

In the wild, the birds enjoy a boundless freedom like that of hardly any other animal. Therefore, they suffer that much more in captivity. It's up to you as bird-keeper to see that these wonderful creatures maintain their joy in living through correct maintenance and feeding.

The Healthy Bird

The Assessment of the Bird

It is important for every bird fancier to be able to assess the *health status* of his animal. This isn't so easy, for birds are masters at the concealment of disease symptoms. Apparently healthy, they can nevertheless be very gravely ill. When you finally really see that something is wrong, it is often too late. This behavior of the bird is a natural defense strategy, for predators try first to catch the weak birds in a flock. If a bird were to give signs of his weakness, he would immediately become the target of attack. Therefore, with birds it takes much more observation than

With shining eyes, this beo takes in his surroundings. He doesn't give the impression of being ill.

Health Check

Behavior
healthy	active, takes interest in surroundings
ill	not very active, sits quietly, also keeps head tucked in all day

Plumage
healthy	smooth, shiny, full
ill	slightly ruffled, with bare spots

Eyes
healthy	shiny, open
ill	dull, half-shut

Food and Water Intake
healthy	normal
ill	irregular

Elimination
healthy	color and consistency normal (see page 9)
ill	too soft, too hard, abundant fluid

Beak
healthy	smooth, without deposits
ill	cracked, brittle, with deposits, misshapen, soft

Nose
healthy	smooth, without discharge
ill	rough, with discharge, discoloration, stuffed nostrils

Legs, Toes
healthy	smooth, without deposits
ill	thick scales, crusts, gray deposits, swollen, thick, black toes

with other animals to distinguish between the healthy and the sick. The adjacent table can give you some points to go by. Also, the *nutritional state* gives important information about health. When you feel the breast of the bird, the musculature should be firm and round. The crest of the breastbone should not protrude sharply.

Parrots

The parrots include the true parrots along with the parakeets, the cockatoos, and the lorikeets. They have a very sturdy, hard, movable *beak*. In a healthy bird there are no remnants of food on the beak or in the corners. No swellings are to be seen under the eyes.

The excreta consist of firm feces with the masses clearly distinct from one another, creamy white urate (see page 123), and very little clear, fluid urine. While smaller species drop feces 25 to 50 times per day, the larger species, like aras, are content with 8 to 15 times per day.

The parrots love to climb and fly; some are good imitators. The *social birds* show strong participation in their surroundings, love playthings, and can become very tame. However, if an otherwise shy bird suddenly appears friendly, it can be a sign of illness.

Parrots need a lot of company and occupation to stay healthy.

Feces are regularly excreted and are of a rather runny consistency. The whitish urate portion (see page 123) is clearly distinguishable.

Grain Eaters

Among the so-called granivores are the canaries and other finches, waxbills, weaverbirds, and buntings. They are generally livelier than the parrots and have a *high-exercise requirement*. With much patience, some species can become quite trusting, but they never become as tame as parrots. When you try to catch one of these restless fellows, he will always fly away in fright. If he just stays sitting there, he is most certainly sick.

Soft-Food Eaters

Soft-food eaters like hill mynas or nightingales are *very lively* and *demanding* animals. They need a lot of space for hopping and flying, but they also like to hide in shrubbery. Except for a few species (e.g., hill mynas) they remain rather shy.

Food and excreta are scattered all around. The latter are soft to thinly fluid; however, you can clearly distinguish between feces and the urate portion (see page 123).

Health Precautions

or get veterinary help. Delays can quickly lead to death. If a new bird comes into your collection, it should be isolated for at least six weeks before it is put into the aviary with the others.

Parrots and hill mynas should be taken to a veterinarian at least once a year for a *health checkup;* for more sensitive species this is too stressful.

The Regular Health Precautions

To differentiate sick from healthy birds, *daily, thorough observation* is strongly recommended. A tame bird can be carefully taken in the hand for this. A shy grain or soft-food eater should only be observed for suspicious signs because these birds are made too anxious by being caught, and an illness can develop from this stress alone. The goal of the daily inspection is to recognize the very first signs of a disturbance in health and to undertake the proper procedures

Prevention of Ectoparasites

Birds that are kept singly in the house fortunately rarely suffer severe attacks by ectoparasites (see page 66). With birds kept in an aviary, on the other hand, the parasites can often increase so much as to be life-threatening. To decrease the risk of infection, the aviary should be built in such a way that your caged birds have no contact with wild birds. You should spray large cages or aviaries at least once a month with an organic, nontoxic mite spray like Exner Petguard;

In such a throng, any bird quickly goes into a panic and suffers a thousand anxieties.

Dangers of Free Flight

✓ Poisoning from plants, chemicals, cleaning materials, table salt, cigarette butts, or metals
✓ Burns from hot stove burners, open pots, lamps, or lighted candles
✓ Injuries from flying against windows
✓ Drowning in bathtubs, toilets, buckets, watering cans, or flower vases
✓ Catching delicate toenails in curtains
✓ Electrocution from gnawing on electric wires
✓ Strangling in strings or threads
✓ Getting caught on insect glue strips
✓ Dogs and cats

it is not harmful to the birds, but it nevertheless destroys mites very effectively.

In the summer it is advisable to examine aviaries once a week with a magnifying glass for parasites, especially in corners and cracks. Fallen feathers should also be inspected.

Prevention of Endoparasites

Infection of a bird with endoparasites (see page 53) usually takes place via food or water. In order to prevent the spread of these parasites, you should

● Protect food and water dishes from contamination with feces
● Change contents daily
● Renew bath water daily
● Remove excrement daily; with soft-food eaters twice daily
● Regularly clean the cage's floor and equipment

Garden aviaries should always be roofed so that the inhabitants cannot be infected by the feces of wild birds.

You should have a sample of the birds' feces tested for parasites by a veterinarian every three months. A general worming is not advisable, because many endoparasites can only be destroyed by very specific medications. Endoparasites should *not* be treated by natural health care methods.

Vaccinations

There are only a few vaccinations available for pet birds. Theoretically, there is a possible vaccination against *Newcastle disease* (see page 122) for songbirds and parrots; however, its effectiveness is disputed.

Birds kept in a cage should be allowed to fly free regularly. Clear away all sources of danger first.

Finch and canary populations should be vaccinated against *canary pox* (see page 123) annually at the beginning of July. There is no vaccine available for parrots.

You should discuss with your veterinarian whether any vaccinations are available and advisable.

Avoiding Sources of Danger

It is important for the maintenance of good health to remove *all sources of danger* from the vicinity of your bird. Many birds come to grief during free flight just because of their confidence and curiosity.

Correct Maintenance

Because of its ability to fly, the bird is used to almost limitless freedom in nature. When you take such an animal into the house, you undertake great responsibility for its well-being. The bird in captivity is completely dependent on your attention, your knowledge about its requirements, and your care.

The Torture of Choosing

Whether cheerful grain eaters, sensitive and fussy soft-food eaters, or trusting, demanding parrots—the choice is huge, and the bird fancier won't have an easy time deciding. *Don't buy any wild-caught birds!* Such a bird, snatched from its home territory, probably even from its partner, is

The budgerigar needs a daily bath to feel comfortable and maintain its feathering.

The Most Important Care Measures

Measure	Parrots	Grain Eaters	Soft-Food Eaters
Fresh food and water	daily	daily	twice daily
Cleaning thorough	every 2–3 days	every 2–3 days	daily
quick	daily	daily	twice daily
Spraying with Organic Insecticide			
plumage	weekly	weekly	weekly
cage	monthly	monthly	monthly
Careful observation	daily	daily	daily
Careful inspection	weekly	as needed	as needed
Claw and beak care	as needed	as needed	as needed
Fecal examination for parasites	every 3 months	every 3 months	every 3 months
Facilities for bathing	daily	daily	daily
Spraying	daily (especially for parrots from rain forests)	—	—

always sad and anxious. It will probably never feel at home with you. On the other hand, birds that are raised in captivity—assuming they are properly kept—develop into wonderful friends. You should also avoid wild-caught birds for reasons of species protection.

Birds always feel best in a natural habitat.

Being social creatures, birds—especially parrots—need a partner and should never be kept alone.

In making a choice of species, you should consider the following points:
- How much space can you give the bird?
- A very close relationship is only developed in certain parrot species and hill mynas, but these birds also make demands on the owner. You must have enough time to pay a lot of attention to them many times daily.
- With a large parrot like an African gray parrot, ara, or cockatoo, you must be clear that it will be a relationship for many decades. These birds grow old and bond to their partner for their entire life, and also to their caregiver. They are highly intelligent and sensitive and need a great deal of attention and stimulation but also, because of their dangerous beaks, good training.

- Smaller species are easier to keep. However, they are not all as tame as the budgerigars or cockatiels. Because of their extremely fluid feces, the lorikeets are problematical, as are the hill mynas.

No Lone Birds, Please

Birds are social animals and should *never* be kept by themselves. No matter how much attention you give the bird, you can never really replace a bird partner. Your bird, who thinks of you as a partner, will be constantly frustrated. From this situation many *psychological disorders* and *physical ailments* can develop; birds can even pine to death from loneliness and grief.

With a suitable partner these problems never arise.

If you want distinctly tame birds (parrots, hill mynas) and a close relationship to them, you should first aquire one young bird and spend a great deal of time with it. Then, a few weeks later, a second nestling can be added and slowly acclimated.

Children and Birds

The ideal friends for children are budgerigars and cockatiels. Here the same rule also applies: never keep just one bird!

Even if the care can already be taken over by older children, you must see to it yourself daily that the birds lack nothing.

The Right Housing

The best shape for housing is without question the one with the *greatest possible room for flying*, and both garden or indoor aviaries or a bird room offers this. These birdhouses can be very decoratively arranged with nonpoisonous shrubs, tree trunks, plants, and stones. Under no circumstances should you chain parrots to an open perch!

The Right Cage

Unfortunately, not every bird fancier has the space requirements for a large aviary. If you keep your birds in a cage, you should make sure it is the right size and form. Completely unsuitable are round birdcages or elaborate constructions. The best shape is a simple rectangle, which for birds like buderigars or canaries should have a minimum size of about 24 × 12 × 20 in (60 × 30 × 50 cm) (length × width × height), but a better size would be 39 × 20 × 32 in (100 × 50 × 80 cm). For larger birds the cage must be

correspondingly roomier. With budgerigars, which climb a great deal, the cage should be taller, whereas with soft-food eaters it should be longer because they need space to hop.

The grillwork or cage grate must be free of toxic materials because, otherwise, parrots can poison themselves by gnawing on the bars.

The Arrangement of the Cage

Three to four perches are usually enough but some of the perches can be exchanged for branches of natural wood (e.g., fruit trees, willow, oak, alder, or poplar). The usual plastic or wooden sticks can cause sores on the ball of a foot. The branches should be of varying strengths and thick enough so the bird can grasp them with his toes about two-thirds or three-fourths of the way around. Before you introduce the branches to the cage, you should scrub them under hot water. For parrots, the natural wooden branches are an important means for activity; they love to gnaw on them.

It is also important that at least some of the perches be springy.

● You need enough food dishes so you can give each different kind of food in a different dish. Thus, you can tell better what foods your bird likes.

Cage Equipment

- Natural wood branches, wooden perches
- Container with grit or crushed mussel shells (for grain eaters)
- Limestone or cuttlefish saucer
- Small bathhouse or bird bath
- Playthings (only for parrots)
- Sleeping boxes, primarily for parrots
- Enough water and food dishes

To avoid ulceration of the feet, you should use perches of natural wood.

Larger parrots need at least this cage size—and additional free flight.

Automatic feeders are not recommended. The bracts of the grains can block the opening, and the birds can starve in front of the full feeder. Automatic waterers, on the other hand, are very practical.

Never feed fruit and soft food on the ground. Instead, put a sufficient amount in a dish in a raised position.

● Use sand or newspaper as a bottom cover.

The Right Location

Wherever you spend most of the time is where the birdcage should be placed—with the exception of the kitchen, because there are too many dangers lurking there. Your bird will feel the best in a bright location near a window. However, drafts and full sunshine must be avoided. Sun-light is important, of course, but the bird must be able to withdraw into the shade. Cigarette smoke and loud music are injurious to your bird's health!

Free Flight

For all birds kept in a cage, it is absolutely necessary that they be allowed to fly free for several hours daily, but for one hour at the minimum, in order to provide them with enough exercise. Otherwise, the birds will get fat and become sick. Aviaries must offer them sufficient flying space.

Important: Build a bird tree for your birds' free flight with a large saucer to catch their droppings.

Proper Diet

In the wild, a bird can seek the food that best meets its needs. Caged birds are dependent on what you offer them. Their health depends on how well you have familiarized yourself with your charges' food needs and, also, on how ready you are to feed in accord with them.

The Most Important Nutrients

Protein, carbohydrate, and fats, the content of amino acids, minerals, trace elements, and vitamins, and the digestibility for the bird constitute the value of a food.

Protein is obtained by the bird from both vegetable and animal foods. However, vegetable protein differs from animal protein in the combination of amino acids. Many of these are es-

sential for life and must be accessible to the bird in its food. Generally speaking, animal protein contains more essential amino acids than vegetable protein. This deficiency in vegetable food can be compensated for to some extent with a

Vitamin Deficiency Diseases	
Deficiency in	**Consequences**
Vitamin A	Body lacks resistance to infection Diseases of upper respiratory tract, of kidneys Disorders of bone development Hyperkeratosis Feather discoloration, eye changes Motor disturbances Reproductive problems
Vitamin D$_3$	Disturbance of calcium-phosphorus metabolism Bones: rickets, osteomalachia Soft beak, paralytic symptoms, thin-shelled eggs
Vitamin E	Central nervous system disturbances Motor disturbances Liver damage Infertility
Vitamin B	Motor disturbances, convulsions, paralyses and growth retardation, turned toes, swollen feet Fatty liver Poor hatching
Vitamin K	Reduced blood coagulation

A balanced and varied diet is vital for birds.

widely varied diet. In periods of higher protein requirement (molting, brooding, growing), all birds—even grain and fruit eaters—fall back on animal protein such as insects.

Carbohydrates, the main components of plants, are used by birds to cover their energy requirements; they are relatively easy to digest. On the other hand, the raw fiber they also contain is mostly indigestible for birds. Therefore, many birds, especially the parrots, hull the seeds and remove the skins from nuts and fruits before consuming them.

What the bird body doesn't use immediately for energy is stored as fat.

Fats supply more than double the energy that the same weight of carbohydrates provides. Birds in the wild store up a fat deposit for times of need (winter, long periods of drought), but that is regularly used up. In caged birds, however, this depletion of fat stores often does not take place; thus, severe health problems can result.

But fats are also necessary as carriers of fat-soluble vitamins A, D, E, and K and the essential fatty acids. At brooding time sufficient provision of essential fatty acids is a prerequisite for a good hatching rate.

Vitamins are all irreplaceable for maintaining life processes. Vitamin deficiencies lead inevitably to malfunctions and illnesses (see table, p. 17). Unfortunately, in ornamental birds, neither the exact vitamin requirements nor the vitamin content of their food is known. But it is known that, in general, the ornamental birds have a high need for vitamins, especially for vitamins A, D_3, and B, and that it increases in heat and cold, with stress (e.g., transport, change of dwelling), at breeding time, during molting, and with parasitic attack.

Fruit juices are valuable sources of vitamins. They can be given regularly to all birds.

A vitamin excess would also be harmful, of course, but the main cause of disease in caged birds is an inadequate supply. Providing enough vitamins by means of the ordinary food can hardly be achieved in cage maintenance. Furthermore, the vitamin content of the food drops markedly with long storage. Therefore, supplementary vitamins must be provided.

Deficiency in	Arises Through
Vitamin A	feeding grain exclusively
Vitamin D_3	no direct sunlight (windowpanes absorb UV!)
Vitamin E	rancid food

Budgerigars get a part of their requirement for vitamin B_{12} by ingesting their own feces. Because vitamin K_2 is partially formed by microorganisms in the intestine, it is particularly necessary to administer the vitamins B and K after a course of antibiotics or sulfonamides.

Minerals and trace elements compromise a list of elements that function in building the body. Some are necessary in larger quantities (e.g., calcium, phosphorus, potassium, sulfur, magnesium), others only in traces (e.g, manganese, iron, zinc, iodine, copper, cobalt). Unfortunately, at this time there exists no exact information about the mineral requirements of the ornamental birds. Therefore, sources of minerals, such as cuttlefish and mussel shells, or grit should always be available to the birds so they can take what they need.

Sources of Vitamins and Protein

Greens or green food
● Leaf and flower buds, as well as leaves of fruit trees, hawthorn and sloe, maple, birch, alder, oak, beech, elm, willow, elder, Scots pine, spruce, and huckleberry and blueberry
● Stinging nettles, all types of lettuce, dandelions, parsley, brussel sprouts, spinach, sorrel, chickweed, fresh sprouts.
Fruits/Vegetables
● Peeled tropical fruit, such as oranges, bananas
● Raisins (unsulfured!), figs, grapes, apples, pears
● Mountain ash berries, pyracantha (firethorn) berries, blackberries, raspberries, elderberries, currants
● Melons, sweet cherries, apricots
● Tomatoes, cucumbers, carrots, celery
Animal protein
● Living animals like worms, pill bugs, fruit flies, mealworms, fly maggots, crickets, smooth caterpillars, spiders, aphids, insects of conifers, tubifex, water fleas, grasshoppers, snails
● Eggs (hardboiled only), skim-milk cottage cheese
● Good soft food (pet store dealer) and mixed foods for poultry, for example, for chicks or laying hens

Fresh fruit should be on the menu, especially for fruit eaters like the beo.

Important: Too many mealworms are harmful! Offer only freshly skinned animals in small quantities.

Earthworms are too tough for small birds, and, besides, during the reproductive season from May to July, they are poisonous.

Snails and earthworms serve as intermediate hosts for parasites of birds (tapeworm and gapeworm). Therefore, have the feces examined regularly!

Water

Naturally, birds need water too. But the quantity varies widely according to their origins and their diet. Fruit eaters take in much fluid with fruit. Even seeds contain about ten percent water. Also, with the breakdown of fats and carbohydrates, the birds generate some water internally. Some species are able to go all day long without additional water if necessary. If the water of-

Millet is a special treat that can always be offered to the bird.

Parrots need something to gnaw on constantly. This one has caught himself a pinecone.

fered them is not to their liking, they simply leave it there. Therefore, you cannot rely on the birds' ingesting medications, vitamins, or minerals via their drinking water.

Spoiled Food

Greens and animal protein must always be served fresh because they go bad very quickly. But grain food can also be spoiled by being kept too long and by dust and moisture. Oily seeds and fats very quickly become rancid. In addition, food mites can nest in food or fungus can spread through it.

Spoiled food must not be used because it can cause severe health problems, such as digestive disturbances or liver damage. Usually, you can't tell by looking at it that the food is spoiled. Therefore, you should sample seeds and grains every so often or examine the food with a magnifying glass and all your senses.

Have the food examined by the veterinarian from time to time. He can also do a culture for fungus.

Food to Grow On

Each bird group has special preferences as to food on which to raise their young, but they all feed a lot of animal protein (insects). When your birds are raising young, offer them a feed of fresh skim-milk cottage cheese that is mixed with insects, flies, spiders, and good soft food, possibly skinned mealworms, a hard-boiled egg, and finely grated carrots, besides vitamin and mineral supplements. For parrots and grain eaters, you can also stir in crumbled zwieback or multigrain baby food as a powder (without milk).

Important: Don't feed too much at once, but rather, give less at shorter intervals. The nestlings will stop eating immediately with noise or if they are startled.

Food Ingredients for the Individual Bird Groups

As different as the individual bird groups look, their digestive systems are just as specialized. Unfortunately, there is little more than basic information available about it. Furthermore, eating habits undergo a seasonal change. By using feed rich in variety, you can decrease the risk of providing a faulty diet.

Feeding mistakes increase susceptibility to disease, listlessness, and decreases in reproduction. Therefore, you should thoroughly inform yourself about the eating habits of the bird species you keep. Only then can you offer them an appropriate substitute for their natural diet.

Parrots
● Basic diet (widely varied and good for the beak): seeds, grains, and wheat, e.g., basic feed mixture from the pet dealer

Parrots love grapes, but they shouldn't receive too many of them.

● Legumes, grains, grass seeds, and oilseed also in semiripe or sprouting condition
● Unsprayed, easily digestible green food, fruit, and vegetables
● Fresh wood with buds and bark
● Animal protein like cottage cheese, boiled egg, snails, worms, little meat
● Laying hen mash is also suitable

Grain Eaters
● Oilseeds (e.g., canaries), grass seeds (e.g., waxbills)
● In addition to basic feed, unsprayed green plants and their seed stalks
● Insects
● Fruit and vegetables
● Egg food and food for soft-food eaters

Important: Always take the nutritional status of the bird into consideration when you are fixing its food.

The Most Common Feeding Mistakes

✓ **Overfeeding**
Food that is too rich in energy-producing elements, with too high a carbohydrate and fat content, coupled with too little exercise leads to excess weight.

✓ **Monotonous Diet**
It quickly leads to deficiency conditions.

Both kinds of feeding errors sooner or later result in a severe illness or the death of the bird. Provide a broad spectrum of plant and animal foods; then your bird can seek out what is right for him on his own. To get birds that have been fed a monotonous diet to change over to a varied one can sometimes demand patience and a number of tricks!

Raising
nestlings by
hand requires
a lot of
time and
knowledge
of their needs.

Important: Make sure the grain eaters have tiny stones (e.g., in the form of sand or grit) available as "tooth replacements."

Insect Eaters
● Main food: living insects
● Soft food (with high content of protein and essential amino acids), e.g., at pet supply stores
● Fruit, finely chopped greens, carrot juice to enrich commercially prepared food
● Skim-milk cottage cheese, hard-boiled egg

Important: These food mixtures spoil quickly once they have been prepared and should, therefore, be fixed fresh several times a day.

Fruit Eaters
● Abundant fruit and vegetables
● Pollen, insects (as a protein source)

Important: To prevent fungus disease, make sure there are enough places available to bathe so the birds can clean their beaks of food remains.

Nectar-eating Birds
Among these are hummingbirds and honey eaters. As a keeper of these diet specialists you should thoroughly inform yourself about their requirements.
● Nectar substitute (pet store)—the sugar content should never be higher than twenty percent and the feeding solution should contain no lactose.
● Flower pollen, insects (as a protein source)

Important: The shape of the drinking tube absolutely must fit the shape of the beak. The drinking tube should be reachable from a sitting position to avoid competitive fights.

An Overview of Natural Health Care Methods

In nature, it is entirely normal that animals with particular metabolic disorders instinctively consume special plants, herbs, minerals, or organisms—thus, treating their illness with natural remedies, as humans also did for thousands of years. Unfortunately, there are only a few *scientific* studies of the use of natural healing methods in animals and none yet of their use in birds. We also do not know what remedies birds seek for particular disorders. But in veterinary medicine, we can draw on a great *wealth of experience* of using natural remedies with animals.

Whereas allopathy (see page 121) combats disease or its symptoms with medications or supplies missing substances, *naturopathy* improves by stimulating the defensive condition of the body's own extant healing power. Disorders are supposed to be controlled from inside out, and, thus, healing is achieved. Naturopathy sees the organism as a whole. It is not a single disease or an individual organ that is treated but the disorder of the entire system, with the goal of a healthy biological equilibrium.

If disease processes are so far advanced that regeneration and regulation are no longer possible, naturopathic methods will no longer work either. Many serious illnesses, such as highly contagious diseases and parasites, should under no circumstances be treated with naturopathic methods only. There are also, of course, urgent reasons for surgical intervention. But parallel with traditional medical procedures, natural remedies can support the healing process.

In contrast to traditional pharmaceutical medicine, there are hardly any side effects known to occur from the use of natural remedies. However, not all natural home remedies are suitable for home treatments of birds. In the pages that follow, only the methods that can be used successfully are described.

Homeopathy

"Like can be healed with like." On the foundation of this thesis, Dr. Samuel Hahnemann (1755–1843) developed *homeopathy* (from the Greek *homoios*—"similar" and *pathos*—"suffering") into an outstandingly successful medical art. It is based on the finding that a substance (e.g., a plant toxin) that produces a particular clinical picture in a healthy human, administered in tiny little doses, heals a disease with the same symptoms.

Dr. Hahnemann recognized that a patient whose system of life forces is out of balance would be susceptible to specific pathogens that cause specific diseases. The goal of homeopathy is to reestablish balance following a state of disorder and to mobilize the body's own healing abilities. This is achieved by precise observation of the disease symptoms (the clinical picture) and the use of the appropriate simillimum (see page 123).

Homeopathic remedies come from plants, minerals, and animals. They are tested for their effectiveness (on healthy people).

Brood care can be also promoted in birds like this ara with natural remedies.

Whereas in phytotherapy (plant healing) the plants are used as they are, homeopathy makes use of the active substances in potentiated form; the effectiveness is increased by dilution, that is, it is potentiated. In this process, one part of the "original tincture" is added to nine parts ethanol or saline solution and shaken vigorously ten times. The result is the potency 1X (X = ten times and C = one hundred times).

Then one part of 1X is again mixed in the same way with nine parts of ethanol or saline solution, shaken vigorously ten times, resulting in the potency 2X. These steps are repeated until the desired potency is reached. (In the C po-

tency, one part of the mother tincture is added each time to one hundred parts of ethanol or saline solution and is further potentiated by the same steps.)

The higher the potency, the more dynamic and deep-reaching the effect can be. Particularly in the care of high potencies, the effect of the remedy is considered to be associated with the energy itself, which was enhanced by succession, rather than from the substance of the medication contained in the remedy.

In general, with acute illnesses, the lower and medium potencies are used (3X to 12X), and with chronic and mental illnesses, the higher potencies are used. According to experience, *potency accords* (see page 116) broaden and deepen the therapeutic effect without causing primary aggravating symptoms.

Homeopathic remedies exist in liquid form as *drops* (in an alcohol base) or as *ampules* (in a saline solution) for injections and drinking. They are also available in the form of globules and tablets that are mostly prepared with lactose.

For *use with birds,* only the *ampule form* is recommended.

Important: A careful distinction must be made between symptoms that constitute a case of homeopathic initial aggravation and symptoms that indicate true aggravation of the disease. In the first case, only a portion of the disease symptoms become more pronounced while the rest of the clinical picture improves. Signs of initial aggravating disease should be considered a positive indication for the effectiveness of the chosen remedy. In the case of a truly worsening disease, on the other hand, all the disease symptoms get worse, and the general status of health declines markedly. If this happens, there must be an immediate change of therapy.

Whereas the healing effect of these substances is extensively checked for human use there are almost no tests of medications with animals, and certainly none for birds. Therefore, we have to try as best as possible to apply what is known from tests with humans to animals.

Classic homeopathy used, as a rule, a single substance of a given potency for any one specific disease entity (single remedy). However, this use requires inordinate amounts of knowledge, and years of study, very precise observation, and correct medication syndromes to be able to treat diseases successfully. With birds it

Birds respond very successfully to treatment with homeopathic combination remedies.

is especially difficult to find the right remedy in the right potency, because many otherwise typical (internal) symptoms, modalities, and constitutional characteristics are not recognizable or classifiable at all in these animals. Therefore, in this book you will rarely find single remedies listed.

Complex Remedies

A successful cure is more easily and reliably achieved with the help of complex remedies. These combination preparations contain a number of homeopathic single remedies and have a broad-spectrum effect. Complex disorders lie behind every illness. The combination remedies support the organism's comprehensive defense processes taking place on different planes in different organs. In the choice of this or that correct remedy, the therapist relies not only on the main symptoms in the medication syndrome (simillimum rule) but primarily on the clinical diagnosis. With frequently occurring organic diseases, there have been shown to be so-called "reliable indications" for particular homeopathic single or combination remedies. This means that certain remedies may reliably be used for common diseases.

Homotoxicology (Biological Therapy)

Based on classic homeopathy, physician Hans-Heinrich Reckeweg (1905–1985) founded *homotoxicology*. He stated that diseases are an expression of the body's defense mechanisms against the attack of toxic and other injurious agents. The body reacts to these injuries (homotoxins) by stimulating its own defense mechanism.

Homotoxicology perceives the acute course of disease as something positive insofar as it prevents a severe chronic illness from becoming established through the stimulation of defenses. This self-healing ability should, through the treatment that stimulates antihomotoxic therapy, neutralize the homotoxins and detoxify them.

Antihomotoxic therapy considers itself an extended version of classic homeopathy. Used in therapy are homeopathically prepared, appropriately blended combination preparations (special preparations, homaccords, composita); homeopathic single remedies in single potencies and as potency accords (injeels), homeopathized allopathic remedies employed for the repair of old therapy damage as catalysts for the improvement of cellular respiration, and nosodes for the detoxification or excretion of toxins. It has been demonstrated that antihomotoxic combination preparations are more effective than the separate application of the various individual components.

According to the teachings of homotoxicology, health is the "freedom from toxins and toxic injuries." Because many ailments in birds are caused by toxic injuries, this teaching is very well suited for therapy. It can be employed without great risk and almost never any side effects.

Bach Flower Therapy

The English physician and homeopath, Dr. Edward Bach (1886–1936), also recognized illness for its positive effect in as much as, according to his view, illness is a path to restore harmony between body and spirit.

With the help of the *Bach Flower therapy* that was developed around 70 years ago, negative emotional and character conditions can be harmonized again. A negative general psychological condition can not only cause organic disease and prevent recovery in humans but also in animals and especially so in caged birds. Experience has shown that the therapy is highly effective in animals. It is especially effective for psychological and behavioral disorders (e.g., anxiety, aggressiveness, acclimation problems, feather plucking) and can help in difficult situations.

The Bach Flowers have the effect of positive regulation of the negative emotional condition and the general state of health. From this there follows, indirectly, a greater resistance against emotionally produced physical disorders. But it would be wrong to hope that organic disease conditions can be cured with Bach Flower therapy. In combination with other therapies, however, they can help to shorten the healing process. Also, Bach Flowers do not compensate for damage that has occurred through incorrect care and maintenance.

Bach Flower therapy involves preparation of essences from 37 different flowers of wild plants and trees and Rock Water from a certain spring as the 38th essence. The positive vibrations extracted from the plants are transferred by dilution into the spring water and conserved with alcohol. The resulting essence concentrates are stored in stock bottles.

The system of the 38 flowers, according to Dr.

Bach Flower therapy is highly effective in treating behavioral disorders and psychological problems, especially in parrots.

Bach, is self-contained and embraces all of the basic negative emotional conditions of human character.

Besides the 38 essences, there is one combination essence, *"Rescue Remedy drops,"* used for emergencies, (see page 120), that can offer powerful first aid through the combined effects of their energetic powers.

The *Bach Flower essences* that are obtainable from health food stores, homeopathic pharmacies, and by mail order should first be diluted for use in humans with bottled spring water. For birds, two administrative routes have proven effective:

● Add one or two drops of concentrate directly to the drinking water.
● Because some birds drink very little or nothing at all, you can also dilute the Bach Flowers (one drop in 1 ml of bottled spring water) and drop it on the head or the skin under the wings. This is usually the most effective method of administering the Rescue Remedy drops.

Visit to the Veterinarian

The first visit to the veterinarian should not take place when the bird is already visibly sick. On the contrary, the veterinarian is also your consultant for general questions about optimal care, feeding, and health precautions. You should regularly obtain fecal tests for parasites (see page 11).

If the veterinarian knows you and your bird, in case of illness, it will often probably be enough for you to get advice and medication and spare the bird the stress of being transported.

Before Going to the Doctor

● If possible, take the bird to the veterinarian in his own cage (unless it is too big). The cage should *not* be cleaned beforehand.
● If there are several birds in the cage but only one is sick, take them *all* in. The other birds can already be infected.
● The cage should only have one or two perches left in, to make catching the patient easier.
● Cover the cage very well to lessen the stress for the bird and to avoid drafts. Carry out the transport as *protectively* as possible.
● Also take along samples of all food, fresh feces, shed feathers, and toys for examination.

At the Veterinarian's

To get to the bottom of illness, the veterinarian will probably want to know a lot from you. It

Questions for the Doctor's Visit

✓ What problem is the bird having now? How did it arise?
✓ When did the symptoms begin?
✓ Are other birds or animals sick?
✓ Has this or any other bird ever been sick?
✓ Has another bird been added within the past six months?
✓ Has there been any contact with other birds/wild birds?
✓ How long have you had the bird?
✓ Where did it come from? (Captive-bred or wild-caught?)
✓ Have you tried any treatments yourself? What?
✓ How does the bird behave at home? Does it respond to its surroundings?
✓ Does the bird eat? How much?
✓ Have you changed the food?
✓ What do you feed?
✓ Has it changed its water intake?
✓ Can the bird also get to other plants or substances or could it have inhaled anything?
✓ Have there been any changes in elimination? What are they?
✓ How old is the animal?
✓ Sex of the bird? Has it mated?
✓ Is a partner or a primary care person absent?
✓ How is the bird kept (cage, aviary, free flight—in the house or outside, free flight with others)?
✓ Where is the cage located (kitchen, living room, natural sunlight, shade, drafts)?
✓ How big is the cage?
✓ How is the cage furnished (type of perches, quality/durability of the toys)?

The drops of a natural remedy are administered to the cockatoo with the help of a plastic syringe.

can't hurt if you think about it ahead of time and even make notes (see checklist).

On the basis of the answers you give, the laboratory results on the samples you've brought, and thorough observation and examination of the bird, the veterinarian will render his *diagnosis* and treat the patient. You should follow the *treatment plan* that he gives you to take home very carefully.

Possibly, the doctor will even want to check his feathered patient again after a few days.

How Do You Find a Veterinarian Who Treats Birds with Natural Healing?

Whether a veterinarian specializes in pet birds is often not on his sign. Information about the specialties of practicing veterinarians can be obtained from the local veterinary societies and from the American Holistic Veterinarian Medical Association (page 128).

You can also ask in the doctor's office whether they like to treat birds and how often they do it.

Important: The smaller and weaker birds can become so upset that, merely by being caught for examination, taken in the hand, and handled, they can die of shock. This accident is tragic but often difficult to be avoided and should not be blamed on the veterinarian! Thus, when possible, such risky patients are often only observed in the cage.

Treating
Illnesses
Yourself

Although you have made every effort in the care and feeding of your feathered friend, it can still happen that your bird will get sick. The more carefully you observe your charge, the sooner you will recognize when something isn't quite right with him. Then the chances are greater that you will quickly identify the illness according to the table on the next few pages and can then cure the bird yourself with the aid of the description of the clinical picture. However, sometimes it is better to consult a veterinarian. If this is the case, it is indicated to you in the appropriate clinical picture. But with almost all illnesses you can also support the healing process by the administration of natural remedies.

Symptom	Possible Causes You May Remedy	Symptoms for Alarm
Increased horny growth on beak and claws	(A) Beak deformation	(A) No food intake, splits and cracks beak softens
	(B) Claw deformation	(B) Can no longer grasp
Scratching nose	Stopped up, discharge occludes nostrils	Shortness of breath, accompanied by gummy eyes, ocular discharge
Scratching eye	Irritation of the eye or eyelid	Redness, swelling of the eyelid, secretions around the eye, foreign bodies, cloudy eyes
Scratching ear	Ear discharge	Reddening, growths, disturbances in balance
Scratching plumage	Parasite infestation, eczema, fungus disease	Bare places, reddened scratched-open areas
Scratching feet	Hyperkeratosis	Dry, crusty deposits, leg swelling
Skin swelling	Bruise, injury	Very bloody, crusty, growths, is picked at
Gnawing on feathers	(A) Quill has not emerged (B) Loneliness, boredom	(A) Bleeding (B) Bare spots
Bleeding	Injury	(A) Generalized disease (B) Abnormal leg or wing position

Possible Diagnoses	Disease Description and Treatment (page)
(A) Dislocation	37
Deficiency condition	
Hormone disorder	
Beak mange/scabies	67
PBFD, doctor visit urgent!	76
(B) PBFD, doctor visit urgent!	76
	43
Cold	16
Vitamin A deficiency	99
Poisoning, doctor visit urgent!	44
Fungus—dangerous infection, doctor visit urgent!	
Eye inflammation	41
Vitamin A deficiency	16
Injury	39
Foreign body, doctor visit urgent!	
Severe infectious disease, doctor visit urgent!	
Ear mites	42
Tumor, doctor visit urgent!	79
Disease of inner ear, doctor visit urgent!	
Mites, bird lice, doctor visit urgent!	66–70
Fungus	71
Eczema	70
Deficiency disease, doctor visit urgent!	
Metabolic disturbance, doctor visit urgent!	87
Parasites, doctor visit urgent!	
Hematoma	
Xanthomatosis, doctor visit urgent!	73
Pox, doctor visit urgent!	74
Feather follicle cyst, doctor visit urgent!	69
Tumor, doctor visit urgent!	79
(A) Feather growth disorder	(A) 69
(B) Feather plucking	(B) 91
(A) Anemia, doctor visit urgent!	
(B) Open fracture	82, 83

PBFD = Psittacine beak and feather disease.

Symptom	Possible Causes You May Remedy	Symptoms for Alarm
Motor disturbances	Injury to feet, wings	(A) Generalized disease (B) Abnormal leg or wing position
Breathing difficulty (dyspnea)	Cold	Opened beak, gasps for air, stretches neck, stressed breathing, sits with feathers fluffed
Doesn't eat	Wrong food, food doesn't taste good	Disturbance of general health, vomiting, diarrhea
Doesn't drink	Water doesn't suit taste or is dirty	Sits with feathers fluffed, diarrhea
Vomiting	Misdirected feeding drive, spoiled food; infectious disease	Sits with feathers fluffed, apathetic, diarrhea
Diarrhea	Spoiled food	Disturbance of general health, failure to drink, diarrhea lasts longer than a day
Urinary changes	—	(A) Disturbance of general health (B) Urine is not produced at all
Straining, unease	Egg laying for the first time	(A) Egg-binding, eggs cannot be laid (B) Swelling of body, generalized disease, dyspnea

Possible Diagnoses	Disease Description and Treatment (page)
(A) Deficiency of vitamins B and E, doctor visit urgent!	16
Rickets, doctor visit urgent!	85
Inflamed joint	84
Gout	59
Bumble foot ulcer, doctor visit urgent!	86
(B) Sprain, dislocation, fracture, doctor visit urgent!	82, 83
Infections, doctor visit urgent!	
Poisoning; tumor, doctor visit urgent!	79
Nerve or brain injury, doctor visit urgent!	
(A) Dangerous infection with virus, bacteria, fungus, doctor visit urgent!	inside back cover
(B) Air cell inflammation, doctor visit urgent!	46
(C) Foreign body, doctor visit urgent!	
(D) Tracheal worms, doctor visit urgent!	46
(E) Iodine deficiency, doctor visit urgent!	46
(F) Heart disease, doctor visit urgent!	47
(G) Blood deficiency, doctor visit urgent!	
(A) Liver damage, doctor visit urgent!	(A) 55
(B) Gastro-enteritis from spoiled food, doctor visit urgent!	(B) 53
(C) Inflammation of jaws and crop	(C) 49, 51
(D) Gastro-enteritis, liver, kidneys, doctor visit urgent!	(D) 53, 55, 57
(E) Foreign body, doctor visit urgent!	
(F) Crop obstruction	(F) 51
(A) Inflammation of jaws and crop	(A) 49, 51
(B) Gastro-enteritis, doctor visit urgent!	(B) 53
(A) Missing partner	
(B) Irritation of mucous membrane in crop	(B) 51
(C) Gastro-enteritis or hepatitis, doctor visit urgent!	(C) 53, 55
(A) Inflammation of stomach, intestine, liver, or kidneys, doctor visit urgent!	(A) 53, 55, 57
(B) Endoparasites	(B) 53
(C) Infectious disease, doctor visit urgent!	
(A) Kidney inflammation, polyuria, doctor visit urgent!	(A) 57, 107
(B) Kidney failure, doctor visit urgent!	(B) 58
(A) Severe egg-binding, danger of shock, doctor visit urgent!	(A) 100
(B) Oviduct inflammation [salpingitis]	(B) 62
(C) Malignancy, doctor visit urgent!	(C) 62

Diseases of the Head and Sensory Organs

Many serious illnesses of the avian organism are present in the head plumage, beak, or the sensory organs of the eyes, nose, and ears. Therefore, much time should be devoted to careful examination of the head area.

The *eyes* are more important for the bird than for most other vertebrates. Even the large eye sockets in the skull are very striking. In many bird species the weight of both eyes is greater than that of the brain.

In essence, the *eyeball* comprises the cornea, anterior chamber, lens, vitreous humor, choroid, retina, and optic nerve. In most birds the iris is brown to black, but in some it is brightly colored. In the gray parrot, the color of the iris changes after the age of six months from blue to yellow.

The eyeball is protected by the upper and lower eyelid and the third eyelid (nictitating membrane). The lower eyelid is larger and more mobile than the upper. The "eyelashes" are formed by a row of small bristlelike feathers. The eyelids are moved by muscles and distribute the glandular secretions over the cornea. The visual capability of most birds is not affected when the nictitating membrane is drawn over the eye. Possibly it serves to protect the eye during flying and bathing.

The *ears* are located at the sides of the head. They are not externally visible. The auditory canal is covered with stiff feathers. These feathers decrease the air resistance through turbulence in flight, decrease the wind noise, and prevent the entry of dirt and foreign bodies. The organ of hearing itself and the organ of balance are located in the ear. Hearing capability is best developed in nocturnal birds.

The *beak* consists of the bony core that is surrounded by a horny bill sheath (keratin). The horn is constantly growing and, at the same time, is being worn down with use. In some birds, the upper and lower beak can be moved toward the cranium. Injury, dislocation, or loss of half of the beak are not uncommon.

The *nostrils* exhibit marked differences among species. In some bird species, like the parrots, the entrances to the nose are covered with a waxy membrane. On the inside the nostrils adjoin the nose muscles and the olfactory mucous membrane. The nostrils play an important role in keeping the water metabolism of the bird in equilibrium. They are a kind of "heat exchanger." The bird can retain large quantities of humidity and warmth that normally are lost during expiration. When a sick bird doesn't want to drink his water because of added medications, he can refuse it for a long time.

The *tongue* is very long and extensible in some species, such as the hummingbird, and in others, such as the grain eaters, thick and short. Birds taste with the taste buds at the back of the tongue and in the throat. In general, the organs of smell and taste play a less important role than those of seeing and hearing.

Changes in the Beak

The beak serves the bird for taking up food and chopping it, for grooming, for raising young, and, in parrots, also as an aid to climbing.

Clinical Picture

(A) The beak is deformed. In older birds the upper beak suddenly begins to grow very markedly. Often the coloration of the horn changes, and the beak becomes brittle. If the lower half of the beak also grows, a clinical picture similar to that of a crossed beak develops.
Usually, only the fine tip of the beak grows. It is male animals that are affected for the most part.
Sometimes increased horn formation or growths occur in area of the beak corners.
(B) The bird has injured its beak. The cracks and splits in the beak can be so deep that dangerous bleeding results. Sometimes half the beak is torn away.
(C) The horn of the beak is so brittle that often sections of the beak break off. If nothing is done, this process can progress so far that the beak breaks off to its base and is completely lost.
(D) The bird suddenly exhibits a malalignment of the upper beak. He refuses to eat, and he can no longer grasp with his beak.

Causes

(A) In many cases the keratin grows faster than the bird can use it; this results in the bill continuing to grow longer. The cause cannot be clearly determined yet. Animals that sharpen their beaks vigorously are also affected. There is discussion of hormonal influences. A deficiency of vitamins, minerals, and amino acids may play a role in the large parrots. Often, though, a dislocation of the beak is also the reason that the keratin consumption is too little.
If the skin around the beak is changed, mange mites or fungus are the cause (see page 41).
If the beak becomes soft and deforms, the trigger may be feather loss syndrome (see page 76).
(B) Often the cause is that the bird has flown against a window or has suffered another sort of accident. Also, bites or careless shortening of the overgrown beak half can result in such injuries.
(C) Fungus and parasites, deficiencies, or wounds with subsequent infection can make the horn brittle.
(D) In parrots the upper beak is not fixed but is movable by means of a joint connected with the head. Therefore, it can—under sufficient force—become sprained or dislocated. The lower beak also has a jointlike suspension.

Self-Help

(A) Because the beak grows quickly, it must be trimmed regularly (with some budgerigars every four weeks), otherwise the animal cannot eat properly anymore, doesn't groom, and can injure itself.
The first time it's better to have a veterinarian show you how to do the trimming. With a high-speed precision drill, like those used by manicurists and model builders, it is possible to do a good shaping. Also, other deformities can be smoothed with it. You can also undertake less extensive beak corrections with a file.

Important: Work on the beak must be undertaken very carefully, so the sensitive nerves and blood vessels are not injured. Not recommended is trimming with clippers, because the beak can split.

Horny growths in the corners of the bill can be carefully dissolved with iodoglycerine 1:5 and removed. The treatment is carried out over several days.

(B) Bleeding is stopped with ferric chloride. Until it is healed, the bird should receive soft food (see page 115) and additional doses of vitamins.

(C) If parts of the beak have broken because of brittle horn, the beak is carefully ground and smoothed with the fine polishing machine. Remove peeling scales carefully. Also, paint the beak and the base daily with iodoglycerine 1:5. Make sure that the bird receives sufficient fresh food, vitamins, and minerals.

Important: (D) Under no circumstances attempt to bring the dislocated or sprained jaw sections into normal position again yourself.

● **Natural Remedies**

(A) For abnormally long growth of the bill, a mixture of Graphites-Homaccord and Hormeel is often effective to retard or improve the condition. Give the bird two drops daily.
You can promote the removal of horn buildup at the corners of the beak by administering two drops of a mixture of equal parts of Traumeel, Cutis compositum, and Carduus compositum twice daily.

(B) The immediate administration of one to five drops of Traumeel produces good results.

(C) Mix Sodium-Homaccord, Graphites-Homaccord, and Psorinoheel in equal parts, and administer two drops daily.

When Should You Go to the Veterinarian?

With a sprained or dislocated beak section, you should go to the veterinarian at once! The same goes for deep splits and cracks and if large chunks of the beak are torn away or broken. Also, the development of swellings in the beak absolutely must be brought to the doctor's attention. It could be a malignant tumor.

What Will the Veterinarian Do?

The veterinarian will try to bring the beak back into its normal position.

With deep splits and cracks or a break in the beak, he will try (under anesthesia) to reposition the parts with a stainless steel fine wire. Over time any missing parts can be replaced with plastic paste or a prostheses.

If the upper and lower bills are both missing, the veterinarian will probably put the bird to sleep painlessly in order to spare it death by starvation.

Prevention and Aftercare

Only undertake extensive beak trimming when you have the appropriate grinding machine available and are able to handle it well.

Regularly give your bird fresh branches from elderberry bushes, apple trees, willow, or other nonpoisonous trees. They promote the natural wearing down of the beak. See to it that your bird regularly receives enough vitamins, minerals, and amino acids in its food or drinking water. Try to avoid situations in which the bird can injure itself, such as in an impact against a mirror or window.

Species Susceptibility

Budgerigars display beak deformations relatively frequently and especially the marked overgrowth of the upper bill.

In cockatoos sometimes both beak sections overgrow.

Because the parrot's beak—in contrast to the corn and soft-food eaters—is articulated with the skullbone, the birds in this group often have dislocations (luxations) and sprains (distortions) of the beak. Also, canaries and other grain eaters are known to have malformations of the beak (as in crossed beak). Sometimes the lower beak grows overlong in these species.

Eye Changes

Birds need their eyes for their orientation more than most other animals. Therefore, it is very important to observe for the smallest signs of illness and preferably to consult a veterinarian as soon as something unusual is noticed.

Important: The most common eye symptoms appear as accompanying symptoms with other illnesses, like infections, deficiency disorders, and injuries.

Clinical Picture

(A) Sometimes abscesses form under the eye, on the lower eyelid. The skin clearly bulges out. A yellowish matter shows through. The bird is nevertheless lively.

(B) The cornea, tear glands, tear ducts, and conjunctiva dry out. Then there is the risk of a serious corneal injury.

(C) The third (inner) eyelid (the nictitating membrane) has dropped. It is swollen and red. The eye tears, and the bird tries to scratch it and rub it.

(D) The cornea is cloudy or the iris has changed color. There are changes visible in the pupil, and the lenses are cloudy.

(E) Growths appear on the eyelid.

(F) The bird is suddenly blind. It moves uncertainly in its cage, can no longer find its food, and bangs against walls and obstacles in free flight.

Causes

(A) The reason for the production of abscesses is unknown.

(B) The drying out can be the result of a massive vitamin A deficiency.

(C) The dropping of the third eyelid is usually occasioned by a foreign body.

(D) Often these symptoms appear after an infection or an injury.

(E) The causes of growths and swellings are not clear.

(F) Sudden blindness appears without an externally recognizable cause. It is the result of brain tumors through which the optic nerve is damaged. The disease is incurable.

Self-Help

(A) Cover the abscess with Traumeel eye ointment. Don't get any ointment in the eye while you are doing it—it burns at first.

(B) For two weeks give an increased dose of a good multivitamin preparation with a high vitamin A content.

(C) Try to carefully remove the foreign body. In the case of (D), (E), and (F), self-help measures are not advisable.

● **Natural Remedies**

(C) After removal of the foreign body, infuse one drop of a mixture of Traumeel and Belladonna-Homaccord in the eye three times a day.

For support in all the clinical pictures, you can give two drops of Arsenicum album-Injeel daily.

When Should You Go to the Veterinarian?

In cases (A), (B), (D), (E), and (F) you should consult a veterinarian immediately.

Also, in case (C) you usually will need expert help to remove a foreign body from an eye.

Prevention and Aftercare

Sufficiently high provision of vitamins, especially vitamin A, helps avoid infections and the danger of drying.

Species Susceptibilities

Budgerigars appear to be affected more than other species by abscesses, formation of tumors, and sudden blindness.

In native finches and canaries, cataracts resulting in slow blindness are a frequent accompanying sign of age. However, the birds can usually find their way around in familiar surroundings.

Vitreous Humor Hemorrhage

More than a third of the birds that have an accident exhibit massive bleeding in the vitreous humor afterwards.

Clinical Picture

Vitreous humor hemorrhages are not visible externally (with the naked eye). The hemorrhages can become so massive that a bird can bleed to death.

Important: After severe trauma, such as a crash against a mirror or windowpane, a vitreous humor hemorrhage must be taken into consideration, especially if the bird is stunned.

Causes

A blood vessel is broken inside the eye as a result of a trauma.

Self-Help

● **Natural Remedies**

Immediately instill one drop Traumeel in the eye, avoiding touching it.

In addition, administer two drops Traumeel by the beak. Repeat the instillation and the oral administration about every thirty minutes, then two times per day on the following two days.

● **Bach Flowers**

In addition, against shock, administer one to two drops of Rescue Remedy in the daily drinking water.

When Should You Go to the Veterinarian?

As soon as you have treated the bird with Traumeel for first aid, you should have the doctor look at it.

Prevention and Aftercare

Prevent the possibility of injury to the bird during free flight.

Inflammations of Conjunctiva and Eyelids

Inflammations of the eye in birds are almost always a sign of a more serious disease.

Clinical Picture

The eyelids and the conjunctiva are red and swollen, and the crack between the lids is often closed. The bird scratches at the eye with its toes. Sometimes it tries to quell the irritation by rubbing its eye on the perch. The edges of the lids are very gummy and the feathers around the eyes are stuck together.

Causes

Often eye inflammations occur as an accompanying symptom of severe bacterial infections, such as salmonellosis, mycoplasmosis, Newcastle disease, Marek's disease, mycosis, panophthalmitis, Pacheco's disease, pox, and ornithosis/psittacosis, as well as infections with Pasteurella multocida or Pseudomonas.

Drafts, wounds, chemical irritations, or foreign bodies are relatively rarely the cause of conjunctivitis and lid inflammations in birds.

Important: At the least suspicion of ornithosis or psittacosis, it is imperative that the bird be seen by a veterinarian immediately. These diseases are highly infections to humans.

Self-Help

Because inflammations in birds almost always indicate there is a disease with serious implications, you should immediately take your bird to a veterinarian. All the home remedies serve only as support for the treatment provided by a veterinarian.

● **Natural Remedies**

In addition to the doctor's treatment, instill one to two drops of Aconitum Injeel once daily into the eyes, and administer two drops Arsenicum album-Injeel by beak.

When Should You Go to the Veterinarian?

With inflammations of the eyelid or conjunctiva, or with stickiness around the eye, a veterinarian should always be seen immediately.

Prevention and Aftercare

Optimal maintenance conditions (see page 12) and sufficient provision of vitamins, especially vitamin A, can help prevent serious diseases that accompany eye inflammations.

Mange/Scabies and Fungus Infections

Clinical Picture

The eyes are so overgrown with gray, crumbly deposits that they can hardly open anymore. Also, the area around the eye is always severely affected.

Causes

In birds, changes around the eye are often caused by scabies mites or fungus. The parasites can spread when the skin is scratched and the animal's resistance is weakened.

Self-Help

Using a cotton swab, carefully paint around the eye with Iodine-Glycerine 1:5 once a day.

You should perform this treatment until the condition disappears.

Important: Don't let the solution get into the eye!

● Natural Remedies

A positive effect is also produced by instillation of Traumeel in the eye three times per day. Also orally administer two to five drops of a mixture of Cutis compositum, Carduus compositum, and Coenzyme compositum once daily. This activates the metabolic processes and decreases the duration of the illness.

When Should You Go to the Veterinarian?

If after a week there is still no improvement, you should go to a veterinarian.

Prevention and Aftercare

Provide optimal maintenance conditions (see page 12) and a correct, varied diet with vitamin supplements (see page 16).

Diseases of the Ear

Fortunately, diseases of the ear rarely occur. When they do, the ears are not easy to examine.

A symptom of a problem with an ear can be the head held at a tilt.

Clinical Picture

(A) The auditory canal is exposed. A gummy secretion may be present.
(B) Polyplike growths appear growing out of the auditory canal.
(C) The bird exhibits disturbances in balance; it can even fall off the perch.

Causes

(A) Usually scabies mites cause this inflammation.
(B) The cause is unknown.
(C) Balance disturbances give rise to the suspicion of a disorder of the inner ear.

Self-Help

(A) Carefully flushing over and over with Traumeel drop by drop is usually successful. In addition treat the ear and the cage with an organic mite treatment. They are available in pet supply stores.
(C) Sometimes flushing the auditory canal with undiluted Arnica Tincture has a healing effect.

● Natural Remedies

In the cases of (A) and (C) two drops of Traumeel administered orally each day for one week can support the treatment.

In case (B) you can support the necessary surgical procedures through the administration of two drops of a mixture of Galium-Heel and Glyoxal compositum three times per week. After eight days give these drops only once a week for another three weeks.

When Should You Go to the Veterinarian?

The growths in case (B) must be surgically removed by a veterinarian.

Diseases of the Respiratory and Circulatory Systems

Unfortunately, pet birds very often develop respiratory ailments. A distinction is made between diseases of the upper and lower airways.

The respiratory organs of birds are structured differently from those of mammals. The air passes through the nostrils and nose to the upper voice box (larynx) and from there via the trachea to the lower voice box (syrinx, the vocal organ of the bird). In male birds the windpipe is often very elongated and is situated in curves.

The air flows through the trachea further via the two main and secondary bronchi, as well as a branching system of so-called parabronchi and air tubes in the air cells. Most birds have three to four paired and one to two unpaired adjacent air cells. Almost all air cells connect directly with the lungs. The lungs lie adjacent to the spinal column and the ribs.

Breathing takes place in combination with air cells through the rising and falling of the breastbone (wishbone). The air cells serve as bellows, air reservoirs (some contain only used air, others fresh), and organs of balance. The air cells extend into many bones. Therefore, we speak of "pneumaticized bones." The filling of the air cells with air allows the bird to decrease its specific gravity. (The lungs themselves are considerably smaller than those of a mammal of the same size but are about ten times more effective.) Gas exchange does not take place in the air cells but in the walls of the air capillaries that are adjacent to the parabronchi.

Small birds at rest breathe in and out up to one hundred times per minute; on the other hand, large ones breathe in and out only twenty to thirty times per minute. A bird's lungs can exchange up to 130 liters of oxygen per hour.

A number of pathological changes can occur in this complicated and highly effective respiratory system.

Obstruction of the Nostrils

Clinical Picture

(A) Extending from the nasal cere arise brownish horny growths that can become so large that they grow over the nostrils and interfere with breathing.

(B) Gray-white growths cover the nostrils and threaten to block them.

(C) The nasal openings are blocked with secretions and keratin (see page 122). Sometimes the discharges become so hard that the nostrils are completely blocked and more discharges can no longer flow out.

Some birds shake their heads to get rid of the secretions, keep rubbing their nose on the perches, or pick at their nostrils with their toes. Often, in advanced conditions, the eyes are also affected. Sometimes distinct swellings (infection of the nasal sinuses) also appear either in front of or underneath the eye.

If the nose is blocked with mucous secretions (rhinitis), a bubbling noise can be heard during breathing. With a deposit of dry, hard matter there is a crackling or whistling sound with each inspiration. If the process is allowed to continue, it can result in tissue necrosis.

Other symptoms can be: the bird fluffs itself up, sits apathetically on its perch or the floor, doesn't want to eat, sneezes sometimes, breathes through its open beak, exhibits difficulty breathing (dyspnea) in advanced conditions, and sometimes also has diarrhea.

Causes

(A) It has been suggested that these horny growths are triggered by an imbalance of the sexual hormone system or by a vitamin A deficiency.

(B) An attack of scabies mites can lead to this greatly increased formation.

(C) The causes can be multiple. They extend from comparatively harmless colds as a result of drafts or extreme temperatures to chronic sniffles and vitamin A deficiency, irritation of the airway by foreign bodies or corrosive or poisonous vapors, fungus and yeast infections, parasites, to dangerous bacterial, viral, and other infections, including ornithosis/psittacosis, Newcastle disease, and pox.

Self-Help

(A) and (B) The horny layer is carefully removed with a blunt instrument. Suitable for this purpose, for example, are manicure instruments used for pushing back the cuticle. In addition, the places and the areas around them are treated afterwards with Iodine-Glycerine 1:5 daily for one week (case A) and two weeks (case B). In case (B) the procedure can be repeated once weekly for some time as a preventive measure.

(C) Try to loosen the sticky deposits and obstructions of the nostrils with a solution of normal table salt and water and then carefully remove them. Rinsing the nostrils (see page 100) with a normal table salt and water solution is usually gratefully received by the patient. A drop on each nostril is quite enough for small birds.

Also proven to be helpful is spraying with Euphorbium compositum nose drops. The applicator spray head is held against the affected nostril. In very small birds the entire beak and eye can be sprayed without harm. This therapy is performed until the nose is completely clear.

Important: If dried discharges within the nose cannot be loosened after several days of rinsing, they must be removed surgically by a veterinarian. Because severe bleeding may occur with this procedure, you are urgently advised against trying to do it yourself. The same goes for the removal of foreign bodies from the inside of the nose.

Stickiness and stopping up of the nostrils are usually symptoms of colds. (However, these can also be present in light cases without any stuffiness and only a thin, clear nasal discharge.) Put the patient in a warm, draft-free room. Possibly provide for a source of more warmth. In addition, administer a vitamin preparation with a very high vitamin A content.

You can also let your bird inhale chamomile extract. See page 113 for procedure.

● Natural Remedies

(A) Give your bird one drop each Graphites-Homaccord and Cutis compositum once a week by beak. Continue this therapy for three weeks.

(B) Daily administration of three drops of a mixture of equal parts of Sodium-Homaccord, Graphites-Homaccord, and Psorinoheel provides a good chance of a cure.

(C) Give the sick bird one drop each of Euphorbium compositum, Echinacea compositum, and Mucosa nasalis suis twice daily by beak for three days.

If the disease nevertheless continues, which is demonstrated by labored breathing, shaking of the head, whistling or crackling breath sounds, slightly opened beak, rejection of food, and apathy, something must be done quickly. The lower airway may also be involved.

Quickly provide more warmth and at the same time higher humidity in a location that is quiet and utterly draft-free. Orally give one drop each of Echinacea compositum and Euphorbium compositum three times daily. In addition, you can use Euphorbium nasal spray. If the condition has not improved after 12 hours, consult a veterinarian.

When Should You Go to the Veterinarian?

If the clinical picture as described above does not quickly improve, you should visit a veterinarian without delay. This also applies to deposits on the nostrils that will not dissolve, swellings under the eye that do not go down despite your treatment, and all cases of labored breathing and apathy.

Prevention and Aftercare

Keep your bird away from abrupt temperature changes and drafts. Make sure that no irritating vapors (e.g., from overheated Teflon pans) or smells are present in the vicinity of your bird.

Make sure that there is an adequate supply of vitamin A, especially for parrots and grain eaters. Regularly give them a multiple-vitamin preparation with a high vitamin A content. Vitamin A deficiency is one cause of susceptibility to infection in parrots and many grain eaters. Besides grain there should also always be chickweed, green lettuce, or carrots on the menu for these species!

Important: Treatment should be begun at the first symptom of a cold!

Disorders of the Lower Airways

Clinical Picture

Almost all illnesses in the area of the lower airways (trachea, lungs, and air cells) are evidenced by breathing difficulty (dyspnea). The bird tries to get air with labored raising and sinking of the rib cage.

With every inhalation the tail whips noticeably up and down. In severe cases, for instance with pneumonia, the patient gasps for air with open beak, has fluffed up feathers, and sometimes has disturbances in balance (it sways while sitting). It also refuses food, vomits, and loses weight.

Precisely which disease is present is difficult to determine.

Causes

Many pathogens can be responsible for a disease of the lower airways, for example pox (avian diphtheria), Newcastle disease (see back inside cover), coenurosis, Pacheco's disease, leukosis, viral hepatitis, ornithosis/psittacosis (see back inside cover), coccal infection, pasteurellosis, salmonellosis (see inside back cover), coli infection, tuberculosis, mycoplasmosis, and others.

Very often the symptoms are also caused by fungus or yeasts. A noticeable change in or complete loss of the bird's voice may also indicate a dangerous growth of fungus on the syrinx, whereby the trachea is gradually completely filled in, and the bird suffocates within a few days.

Fungus can also settle in the air cells and seriously inhibit their function. Because air cells also surround the digestive system, the bird usually also exhibits loss of appetite and vomiting, accompanied with a dramatic decline in health and appearance.

Birds with weakened resistance or that are in deficiency states are susceptible to the same fungus infections as are birds that are in stress situations. Also, food that is moldy can be responsible for an infection.

When birds cough and, perhaps, also choke and stretch their necks, they may be infected with tracheal worms. The larvae are ingested with infected worms or snails and within six hours migrate from the intestine to the lungs via the bloodstream and from there to the trachea. Birds can also infect one another. In small birds, like canaries and waxbills, there is the acute risk of death by suffocation! With massive attacks the tracheas of larger birds can also be completely blocked. Air cell or tracheal mites occur in many canaries and other finch species, Gouldian finches, and budgerigars. Often they induce pneumonia.

Trichomonas cause a clinging, yellow, cheesy deposit in the jaws and throat.

Iodine deficiency can lead to an enlargement of the thyroid gland that presses on the trachea and thus causes dyspnea.

Also, diseases of other organs, like the heart, liver, or kidneys, as well as egg-binding, can produce very labored breathing.

Self–Help

Move the ailing bird to a warm, quiet, draft-free place.

Carefully clean its living area.

For iodine deficiency add iodine to its drinking water (one drop tincture of iodine in 25 to 30 ml [0.8 to 1.0 fl oz] of water).

Important: Procedures for examination or treatment must be carried out extremely quietly and carefully. Sick small songbirds, in particular, may suffer shock and death from the stress of being caught and taken in hand.

● **Natural Remedies**

With a bacterial or viral disease of the lower airway you may support any necessary medical treatments by giving a bird in the acute stage one drop of Pulmonaria vulgaris-Injeel once daily by mouth until there is improvement.

Engystol (one drop twice daily) may also be helpful with viral disease.

In chronic cases the daily administration of one drop each of Naphthalin-Injeel and Mucosa compositum has proven effective.

Air cell inflammations can be treated alongside the medical treatment with Echinacea compositum, Euphorbium compositum, and Mucosa compositum by administering one drop of each once daily for five days.

● **Bach Flowers**

To promote recuperation, give two drops of Olive from the stock bottle in 100 ml (3.38 fl oz) of drinking water. In acute cases, Rescue Remedy drops can help the bird to regain its health. Give two drops in about 50 ml (1.69 fl oz) of drinking water.

When Should You Go to the Veterinarian?

If you suspect fungal (Trichomonas) or parasitic (eg. worms, mites) infections, a veterinarian must be consulted without fail for confirmation of the diagnosis. Take a fecal sample from the sick bird with you!

Also, symptoms of pneumonia require a fast, but as protected as possible, visit to a veterinarian.

Important: Because there are a multitude of possible causes, a definitive diagnosis is impossible for a lay person. To some extent there is also a threat of contagion to humans. It is always necessary to take the bird to a veterinarian if the clinical picture does not improve within twenty-four hours. For zoonoses see the inside back cover!

Prevention and Aftercare

Strengthen the resistance of your bird by making available sufficient vitamin preparations with high vitamin A content, minerals, and amino acids. Provide appropriate climatic conditions and warmth.

Pay attention to hygiene! Regular washing of the food dishes and changing the floor material in the cage or aviary is important. Avoid having long-standing damp areas in the aviary to prevent the propagation of fungus spores, and don't use any moldy food. Be careful with sprouted feed! You can increase your bird's re-sistance in stress situations with two drops Echinacea compositum given once a week.

Vaccination is only possible for a few diseases, but not for all bird species (see page 11).

Species Susceptibility

Primarily, it is budgerigars that tend to have iodine deficiency and thyroid diseases.

Heart and Circulatory Insufficiency

Important: If there is any suspicion of heart and circulatory disease, special care in dealing with the small patients is required. With capture, examination, or administration of medications, the possibility of shock and sudden heart stoppage must always be considered. Such measures should always be omitted if possible. Carefully observe the bird in its cage, and administer the medications in the drinking water.

Clinical Picture

(A) Blue color in the legs, skin, and the beak can indicate cardiac insufficiency. Also, labored breathing or fast breathing, general fatigue, sleeping a lot, or declining condition are signs of cardiac insufficiency.

(B) With strikingly pale skin we are often dealing with a circulatory insufficiency, shock, collapse, a circulatory disorder, or anemia.

Causes

Cardiac and vascular disorders are often the consequences of infectious diseases and poisonings.

2

(A) Cardiac insufficiency is found in old parrots that are too well-fed and exercise too little. In older songbirds and overweight parrots, hardening of the arteries also occurs.

(B) Circulatory insufficiency as a consequence of anemia can be caused by wounds, coagulation disorders, liver disease, massive mite infestation (see pages 66 to 69), blood parasites or parasites of the gastrointestinal tract. Because the blood volume, at about ten percent of the body weight, is very small, the loss of even a few drops of blood can lead to a circulatory failure.

Self-Help

(B) You must immediately stop the bleeding after injuries by daubing with ferric chloride. For self-help procedures in infection with red or Nordic bird mites see pages 66 and 69.

● **Natural Remedies**

(A) A generalized cardiac insufficiency should be treated with Cactus compositum, Carduus compositum, Coenzyme compositum, and the addition of vitamins and minerals. A supplementary dose of Cuprum aceticum is recommended. Mix the substances together in equal parts and give 1 ml per day in a little water.

Important: Because of the danger of shock and sudden cardiac arrest, direct administration is not appropriate. If the bird has to be transported or examined intensively, it is advisable to administer the four substances the day before in the drinking water.

(B) For strikingly pale skin, mix Cor compositum, Carduus compositum, and Coenzyme compositum in equal parts, and give the bird 1 ml daily in a little water.

For shock, the administration of Aconitum compositum and Arnica 30X or 200X can sometimes still help.

For emotional shock (e.g., after a serious loss), Ignatia 30X or 200x is indicated. If the patient is cold, Gelsemium 30X is given. Also Carbo vegetabilis 200X can be used.

For collapse, a dose of Carbo vegetabilis 200X should be administered every thirty minutes. When the bird opens its eyes, Sulfur 200X should be given every three hours.

In shock or collapse, the preparations named are dribbled into the beak one or two drops at a time.

● **Bach Flowers**

For anxiety and shyness Aspen often helps. If the bird must be transported, ahead of time give it two drops in 100 ml (3.38 fl oz) of drinking water.

Also, the Bach Flower Star of Bethlehem or the Rescue Remedy drops will help a bird to recover from shock. Mix two drops in 10 ml (0.34 fl oz) water and give one to two drops of it every hour.

When Should You Go to the Veterinarian?

When a bird has wounds or it doesn't respond to treatment within two days, it should be examined by a veterinarian. If possible, a fecal sample should be taken along for examination for parasites.

Prevention and Aftercare

Make sure that your bird gets enough exercise and doesn't get too fat.

Make sure through thorough, regular cleaning of the living area that parasites can't spread. For prevention, spray the bird and its cage regularly with organic nontoxic products.

Diseases of the Digestive System

The digestive organs of the bird consist of the beak cavity, esophagus, crop, glandular or true stomach (proventriculus), muscular stomach (gizzard), and the intestines. In general, all the individual organs—according to the bird group (parrots, grain eaters, or soft-food eaters)—are variously large or strongly developed, for the digestive system must cope with very contrasting foods.

The ingested food is mostly swallowed whole and makes its first stop in the *crop.* In most birds this is a simple, serpentine widening or bulge in the esophagus. But here, with the help of the saliva, a softening and a kind of predigestion of the food also takes place. Because this primarily offers an advantage with hard seeds, the grain eaters, such as canaries and budgerigars, have a relatively large crop.

From the crop, the food first goes to the glandular stomach and then the gizzard. In general, the food is chemically broken down in the *glandular stomach* and then mechanically broken down with powerful kneading in the *gizzard.* In the grain- and plant-eating species, the latter is very muscular and provided inside with a firm horny skin. The food is ground by assymetric contractions of the musculature and often is further supported by a hard rubbing plate and ingested grit (see page 122). In the meat-eating species, the gastric juices play a greater role in digestion. In some fruit eaters the gizzard is insignificant.

In some bird species, for example, some water birds, there is even a third stomach section.

The adjacent *intestine* processes the now liquid food relatively quickly. The intestine ends in the *cloaca,* into which the ureters, as well as the sex organs (seminal ducts, oviducts), empty. *Excreta* in birds normally consist of two parts, the white, creamy uric acid and the dark-brown to green feces, the actual stool. In most grain eaters, normal feces are pastelike. In the soft-food eaters, they are rather mushy and of watery consistency.

Metabolism in birds is higher than in mammals. Because the food eaten is digested quickly, birds must eat often. Small bird species do not survive very long without any food intake. Therefore, you must respond immediately when you notice that your birds may have a disorder of the gastrointestinal tract.

Inflammation of the Beak Cavity

The beak cavity is often afflicted with inflammations. It is, therefore, important to notice any changes in the beak cavity during examinations of the bird.

Clinical Picture

The bird doesn't eat at all voluntarily. As a result it can quickly starve to death.

Besides redness and inflammation you sometimes also see a whitish or yellowish coating in the throat area. The tongue can also be affected.

Causes

Redness and inflammation of the beak cavity are usually a consequence of bacterial or viral infection of the upper airway.

Also, scalds or burns from caustic or hot substances can be the cause. Whitish or yellowish coatings can be symptoms of a vitamin A deficiency. But such coatings are also caused by fungi, yeasts, or Trichomonas. Pox infection also causes thick mucoid deposits. Injuries to the tongue can arise from splinters from gnawing on wood or unsuitable playthings. Or there may be strangulations with rubber bands, threads, or hairs.

Self-Help

Feed the bird only with soft food or a fluid diet for the next few days (see page 115). It can also be helpful to mix dextrose into the drinking water. If the bird still doesn't want to eat, you must force feed it, because otherwise it will starve to death. To do this, give it the soft-to-fluid food with the aid of a dropper or spray, drop by drop (see page 112).

A supplement of vitamin A is advisable, even if there are no coatings visible.

● **Natural Remedies**
Give Arnica-Injeel, Mucosa compositum, and Echinacea compositum twice daily (one drop of each) directly in the beak. For wounds or burns, you should also administer one drop of Traumeel.

When Should You Go to the Veterinarian?

If the inflammation has not improved within two days, you should consult a veterinarian. With white or yellow deposits he should be consulted to confirm the diagnosis. With pox or other infectious diseases, an early diagnosis is essential to prevent the infection from spreading rapidly.

What Will the Veterinarian Do?

The veterinarian will confirm the diagnosis and prescribe the appropriate medications for treatment. If a foreign body is the cause, he will remove it.

Prevention and Aftercare

Provide your bird with adequate amounts of vitamin A (see page 16). See to it that it can't get to any caustic fluids or hot food.

Make sure toys are secure against breakage and have smooth surfaces. Give your pet fresh branches to gnaw on.

Crop Inflammation, Crop Obstruction

Normally, the crop is never empty if the bird has had an opportunity to eat. In some species,

3

when the gizzard is empty, the food proceeds immediately to the stomach. You should be aware of this when feeding a famished bird, so that no digestive problems occur (offer small quantities and slowly). With parrots, however, food is "temporarily stored" in the crop first.

In some species the crop milk is formed in the crop; this serves as the main food for the young in the first days of life. In other species the parents first collect the food for their young in their own crops and predigest it into a more easily digested "baby food."

Clinical Picture

The general condition is usually impaired. The animal sits fluffed up in a corner and eats little or nothing at all. There is noticeable choking and vomiting of ropy, slimey matter. Typical of the disorder is that the bird performs a kind of slinging movement of its head so that the feathers of the head are completely covered with mucus and are sticky. In many animals diarrhea occurs at the same time as does dyspnea, with cheeping breath sounds.

On palpation the crop feels enlarged due to the severe swelling of its mucous membrane, although the crop contains little or no food. Sometimes one can feel masses of mucus. The consistency is doughy.

The ailing bird very quickly wastes away.

Crop inflammation can easily recur.

Important: The regurgitation of whitish mucus containing grains need not always be a symptom of a crop inflammation but can also be caused by an exaggerated, misdirected feeding drive, particularly in male budgerigars that are kept alone (see Behavioral Disorders, page 91).

Causes

A crop inflammation can be caused by spoiled, toxic food or by the ingestion of other indigestible substances.

In states of generally low resistance, deficiency, or incorrect use of antibiotics, fungi, yeasts, Trichomonas, or bacteria are more likely to grow and lead to an inflammation of the crop. Also, a crop obstruction can trigger an inflammation. It can result from ingestion of too much food, grit, or sand. The crop is bulging with undigested or indigestible matter. If the bird also takes in water, the grains in the already filled-to-bursting crop swell. The organ becomes overstretched and immobilized. The overloaded crop becomes clearly visible and palpable.

Foreign bodies in the crop are rare. There are also, of course, occurrences of crop inflammations of unknown cause.

Self-Help

Insofar as spoiled food or indigestible or toxic substances may be causes, these must of course be removed immediately.

Feed with a soft diet (see page 115) to which supplementary vitamins have been added.

If the bird will eat absolutely nothing on its own, you must force-feed it with a tonic (see page 114). To stimulate an appetite a gentian root infusion can be added to the drinking water. Chamomile is also helpful as a drinking water additive to relieve the inflammation. With a crop obstruction, you should withdraw food from the bird for twenty-four hours. In addition, you can try to empty the crop by means of very carefully massaging the crop contents. But the procedure is risky, because the frightened animal can easily suffer a shock.

● **Natural Remedies**

Give one drop each of Nux vomica-Homaccord, Mucosa compositum, and Veratrum-Homaccord two to three times daily orally until there is an improvement of the condition.

For crop obstruction, administer one drop of Nux vomica-Homaccord three times a day.

When Should You Go to the Veterinarian?

If the condition does not improve after one to two days, you should go to a veterinarian. He must also help with a crop obstruction.

What Will the Veterinarian Do?

The veterinarian will determine whether there is an infection with fungus, yeast, or Trichomonas or if bacteria are the cause of the inflammation. Then the appropriate therapy can be prescribed.

Often a crop obstruction can only be relieved by surgery or with irrigation.

Prevention and Aftercare

Make sure that the food is not moldy or spoiled and that the bird can't ingest any other indigestible or poisonous substances. Besides providing a varied diet (see page 16), give adequate amounts of vitamins, particularly vitamin A.

Parrots don't need any grit—the contractions of the gizzard are strong enough to grind up the food. On the contrary, grit can be dangerous for parrots. Sick birds tend to swallow too much grit and, thus, overload both crop and gizzard. Instead, offer small parrots crushed oyster shells. They serve to provide calcium and don't lead to overburdening the crop, because they are broken down over time.

Species Susceptibility

Primarily parrots, especially budgerigars, are affected by crop inflammations. Recurrences are quite common.

Gastrointestinal Inflammations

Despite the great differences in the choice of diet and in the digestive systems, the various bird groups display very similar symptoms in the presence of diseases of the stomach and intestine. Diarrhea occurs relatively frequently.

Clinical Picture

The general condition is impaired, the bird sits on its perch apathetically and with ruffled feathers or even sits limply on the floor. It eats very little or nothing at all. Often the abdomen is swollen, and, frequently, the small intestine, the duodenum, is clearly visible through the abdominal wall.

The cloaca (see pages 49 and 106) may be dirty and inflamed.

The feces are thinly liquid, smeary, and mixed with the urine portion; color and smell are altered. They can be brown, green, or yellowish in color and with or without blood intermixed.

Important: If the urine portion is thin, mucous, or thin and watery but the feces themselves still have their usual shape, it is not a matter of diarrhea but polyuria (see page 107)!

Causes

Diarrhea (enteritis) can have many causes. The food can be spoiled by mold, rot, or mites, not suitable for the bird species you have (see page 20), or hard to digest.

Poisoning can also cause diarrhea.

Infections with fungus, viruses, or bacteria, as well as attacks of parasites like worms and protozoa (e.g., *Coccidia* and *Giardia*), can present with diarrhea.

Diarrhea can also be an accompanying symptom of diseases of the liver, pancreas, glandular stomach, or gizzard. With an impairment of intestinal motility, the body also reacts with diarrhea.

Important: Stress or excitement can also cause softer-than-usual feces, as does egg laying. Therefore, not every thin bowel movement must be immediately classified as pathological!

After the consumption of large quantities of fruit, the feces will also appear softer than usual; certain berries or carrots change the color of the stool.

In some species, such as the lory, a thin, watery stool is completely normal because of the amount of nectar ingested as food.

Self-Help

Important: Diarrhea must be treated quickly, because the bird can become dehydrated after a very short time. If your bird drinks, you should offer it chamomile or oak-bark tea, because this counteracts diarrhea. In addition, you should administer a multivitamin preparation and mineral solutions.

Check food for perishability, infestation with parasites, and appropriateness for your bird (see page 16). Change it if necessary.

● **Natural Remedies**

If a faulty diet is the cause of the diarrhea, give one drop each of Nux vomica-Homaccord and Veratrum-Homaccord twice daily.

With an infection, in addition to these, Engystol (one drop twice daily) is helpful.

If either parasites or an acute infection is responsible for the diarrhea, administer one drop each of Nux vomica-Homaccord, Veratrum-Homaccord, Carduus compositum, and Coenzyme compositum twice daily by mouth.

Inflammations of the cloaca (see page 121) are best treated with Traumeel ointment that is applied two to three times daily.

● **Bach Flowers**

In cases of serious digestive trouble, Rock Rose and Rescue Remedy drops are highly effective. Mix two to four drops in 10 ml (0.34 fl oz) of water and administer one to two drops daily.

If parasites are the cause, in addition to the antiparasite medication, the Bach Flowers Crab Apple and Centaury are helpful; use two drops from each of the stock bottles in 100 ml (3.4 fl oz) of drinking water for one week. This will stimulate and strengthen the animal's resistance and regenerate its appetite.

When Should You Go to the Veterinarian?

If there is not an improvement in the diarrhea and the general condition within twenty-four hours, it is essential to get help from a veterinarian. Take a fecal sample for diagnostic purposes, and, if possible, take the patient with you.

If the cloaca is inflamed or prolapsed, immediate veterinary help is also required.

Important: If there is any suspicion of poisoning (see page 99), don't waste any time at all. Get to a veterinarian at once!

What Will the Veterinarian Do?

The veterinarian can determine whether there is an infection with bacteria, a virus, or a fungus present.

An examination of the feces for parasites will show whether endoparasites, such as worms, Coccidia, or other protozoans, have triggered the diarrhea. If so, their eggs or oocytes can be seen in the fecal sample under the microscope.

Important: Parasitic infestation and bacterial infectious should be treated immediately with an effective modern, pharmaceutical medication. It must be administered according to veterinary instructions. Natural remedies may be given along with it for support.

Prevention and Aftercare

Make sure that your bird only receives unspoiled food that is appropriate for it. Even if it loves to nibble on your food: salty, spiced food, as well as alcohol, should be absolutely taboo!

Take care that the bird can't get anything that could be poisonous. Many houseplants (e.g., dieffenbachia, oleander, poinsettia) are poisonous!

Do not spray your bird with an insecticide. It will take in the poisonous substance as it preens its plumage.

Every three months take a fecal sample to the veterinarian for examination for endoparasites. Birds in outdoor aviaries can easily be infected by the droppings of wild birds. Therefore, as a precaution, aviaries should always be completely covered on top.

To strengthen powers of resistance to infection and parasites you can regularly offer the Bach Flower Crab Apple two drops in 100 ml [3.4 fl oz] of drinking water).

Species Susceptibility

Gastrointestinal ailments occur in all bird species.

Disorders of the Pancreas

Disorders of the pancreas usually occur in conjunction with other diseases.

Clinical Picture

The animal constantly loses weight in spite of a markedly increased intake of food. The quantity of feces increases—corresponding to the food intake.

The feces are crumbly, superficially colored light-gray to yellow, and very quickly harden into chalky heaps. The fecal and urine portions can no longer be differentiated. Quantities of starch that left the intestine undigested may be seen in the feces. The course of the disease is chronic; there is almost no chance of cure.

Causes

The causes are not known.

Self-Help

● **Natural Remedies**
In spite of the uncertain causes, you should attempt treatment.

Administer one drop each of Lycopodium-Injeel, Nux vomica-Homaccord, and Veratrum-Homaccord once daily by mouth over a long period of time.

● Bach Flowers

Along with this, the Bach Flower Mustard is recommended. Give two drops of the essence from the stock bottle in 100 ml (3.38 fl oz) over several weeks.

When Should You Go to the Veterinarian?

You should go to the veterinarian for confirmation of the diagnosis.

Liver Diseases

The liver is the most important metabolic organ, and, at the same time, it is the organ of detoxification. Therefore, it is very often involved in diseases of other organs or in infections.

Disorders of the liver in the form of inflammation or fatty liver degeneration occur quite commonly in birds.

Clinical Picture

(A) The liver is enlarged and usually a collection of fluid in the abdomen (ascites) develops. The liver swells up like a balloon, and the fluid is even visible or palpable through the thin abdominal wall.

Accompanying symptoms of a liver disease can be diarrhea and/or vomiting. The feces are colored brownish or yellowish.

When the liver can no longer break down toxins sufficiently, the body resorts to other organs for excretion, such as the skin. Therefore, often skin disorders like poor plumage, itchy skin, and dermatitis (especially in the neck region) indicate liver disorders.

Also, polyuria (see page 123) can point to a disorder of the liver.

On the other hand, a yellow coloration (jaundice) of the skin—a typical sign in humans and many mammals—is rarely observed in birds. Sometimes pigment changes in the plumage, e.g. black tips (melanismus), can be found.

(B) In fatty liver degeneration, besides the symptoms described above, a profound increase in fat is found in the animal. In the breast or abdominal region there are thick, yellowish cushions of fat visible under the skin.

Being overweight makes the birds sluggish, short of breath, and exhausted after a short flight, or they don't fly at all anymore.

Important: In a living animal, the presumption of "liver disease" almost always remains only a questionable diagnosis that can only be confirmed by dissection after the death of the bird.

Causes

The chief cause of liver disease is excessive demand made on the liver as a detoxifying organ.

(A) A disorder and degeneration of the liver can be induced by

—a long list of infectious diseases, caused by viruses or bacteria (e.g., Newcastle disease, Pacheco's disease, psittacosis/ornithosis, salmonellosis, tuberculosis, or leukosis)

—a fungus infection

—indigestible and fungus-infected food and a monotonous, unbalanced diet

—poisons that the bird has ingested directly or taken in through the skin

—worm infestations

(B) Causes of fatty liver degeneration is generally an improper diet with food that is too rich in calories accompanied by too little exercise. However, hypothyroidism (underfunctioning thyroid gland) also results in the same symptoms.

Self-Help

(A) Birds with liver disorders have a diminished appetite or refuse food and water entirely. This leads very quickly to dehydration, even in species that drink little or require little water. You must carefully infuse food and fluid into them in small quantities. The special liver diet (see page 114) is recommended for this.

(B) For overweight birds, decrease the quantity of food and increase the availability of fruit and vegetables.
With hypothyroidism, iodine is added to the drinking water (one drop Iodine to 25 to 30 ml of water).

● **Natural Remedies**

(A) In the early stages of a suspected liver disorder, you can try therapy with Carduus compositum and Coenzyme compositum. Give one drop of each of them once a day directly in the beak.
In advanced stages, choose Chelidonium-Homaccord, Hepar compositum, and Coenzyme compositum; administer one drop of each of them per day by mouth over an extended period.
Also, one drop of Arsenicum album-Injeel per day can help.

(B) With fatty liver degeneration give the bird one drop each of Carduus compositum, Coenzyme compositum, and Hepar compositum once daily over an extended period.
Also, for hypothyroidism you can administer the medications named in the same dosages.

In addition, for thyroid problems, one drop Thyreoidea compositum three times per week can be dropped into the beak.

● **Bach Flowers**
For support in liver damage, you can always give the bird Crab Apple. This Bach Flower helps the body break down toxins and strengthens the powers of resistance. Give two drops in 100 ml (3.38 fl oz) of drinking water.

When Should You Go to the Veterinarian?

With suspicion of a liver disorder with protracted diarrhea and vomiting, as well as refusal of food, you need to see a veterinarian right away to establish the causes.

Prevention and Aftercare

With the right food (see page 16) and sufficient opportunities for exercise you are likely to prevent liver disease. On suspicion of a liver disorder you should offer a special feed (see page 114).

Be careful about using insecticides, other poisons, and medications. These don't belong anywhere near a bird.

Have a fecal sample tested for parasites every three months.

After the bird has recovered from an illness, you can still give it two drops of Hepar compositum once a week for some time.

Species Susceptibility

Fatty liver is primarily found in budgerigars and canaries kept indoors; occasionally larger parrots are also affected. Malignant liver tumors have mostly been found in budgerigars.

Diseases of the Urogenital System

The urinary organs serve the bird for excretion and fluid regulation. Those of birds are very notably different from those of mammals.

In most bird species, the kidneys are present as a paired organ, well-concealed in the recesses of the pelvis. Like the mammals, the birds form a concentrated urine, but it consists of uric acids (semifirm creamy-white urate, see page 123), not of urea, as well as a tiny quantity of clear urine. Urate is formed in the liver, then concentrated in the kidneys, and from there moves through the mucous-membrane covered ureters to the cloaca. Here urine and feces are excreted together; in some species more fluid is removed from the urine in the cloaca. Uric acid, urine, and feces are clearly distinguishable from one another.

The male sex organs include the paired, adjacent, bean-shaped testes, the epididymus (paraorchis), the seminal ducts, and the copulative organ. Some bird species have a retractable penis, others do not. The seminal discharge takes place during copulation through the tip of the phallus into the protruding oviduct of the hen.

In female birds, during the early embryonic phase, only the left ovary with its oviduct develops into a sex organ capable of functioning. The oviduct divides into five sections. The yolk-rich egg is in the oviduct tunnel and the [magnum] surrounded with the stringy-white protein layer. Here the egg also receives sodium, magnesium, and calcium. In the adjoining oviduct passages, the egg is furnished with the keratin-containing double-layered shell membrane. Then it moves to the uterus, the calcium chamber, where it stays for about twenty hours. Here the weight of the egg is doubled by the addition of liquids that leads to the formation of the hard eggshell. Finally, within a few seconds, the finished egg passes through the vagina where it is provided with a thin membrane that seals the pores of the hard shell. Finally, it moves into the cloaca and is laid. The female bird has a storage place for the male sperm from which the sperm can be summoned according to the need for fertilizing.

Kidney Inflammation

An inflammation of the kidneys (nephritis) can be chronic or acute.

Clinical Picture

In a chronic kidney infection, the bird has periodically occurring diarrhea and little appetite; in addition, it is apathetic. Its need to drink increases. There is also dyspnea and unkempt plumage. The general state of health rapidly worsens.

The bird sits with legs spread and leaning back slightly.

On close examination, the diarrhea is different from that in gastrointestinal illnesses. The true feces are normal in form, soft or firm depending on the bird species (see page 9), but the kidney portion is watery and pathologically increased (polyuria). The whitish uric acid (urate) and the urine are mixed together. On a piece of paper or cellulose you can clearly see how runny the urine portion is.

The disease can develop over weeks and months.

An acute kidney inflammation, on the other hand, usually goes very fast and, with very severe disorders of the general state of health, leads quickly to death.

Diagnosis is not certain in a living bird.

One can suspect a kidney insufficiency if there is only very little urine excreted or none at all.

Causes

Kidney diseases can be triggered by
—poisoning with chemicals, medications, metals, salt
—mold
—vitamin A deficiency
—tumors
—shock
—abnormal patterns of drinking water intake
In addition, there are unknown causes.

Self-Help

Give the bird a diet that is low in protein but rich in vitamins (a lot of greens and fruit) and keep it warm.

You should add adequate amounts of vitamin A to the drinking water.

Also recommended is a Tyrode solution (see page 115). Make sure that the bird eats and drinks enough. If not, you must instill the Tyrode solution directly into the beak.

For parrots, jars of baby-food fruit or vegetables have been shown to be helpful.

● Natural Remedies

Kidney diseases should be treated with Cantharis compositum, Berberis-Homaccord, and Engystol. Administer one drop of each of them once a day by mouth for one week.

Also, Arsenicum album-Injeel, one drop per day directly in the beak, can be effective.

At any suspicion of kidney insufficiency, give one drop each of Engystol and Solidago compositum.

● Bach Flowers

To give support, offer the patient two drops each of Star of Bethlehem and Pine in 100 ml (3. 4 fl oz) of fluid for at least four weeks.

When Should You Go to the Veterinarian?

If the condition does not improve within two to three days, you should go to the veterinarian. This is important, because the kidneys can also be affected in psittacosis/ornithosis (see inside back cover)!

Prevention and Aftercare

Make sure that the bird always has enough drinking water at its disposal and that it receives enough vitamin A. The diet should be correct for its species and balanced (see page 16). Too high a protein content in the diet can contribute to kidney problems. Never feed moldy food.

Make sure that your bird cannot ingest any salty snacks, poisons, chemicals, medications, metal foils, tin or zinc, tinsel, or poisonous plants.

Species Susceptibility

Kidney inflammations can occur in all bird species.

Tumors of the kidneys (see page 79) are seen in budgerigars comparatively more often than in other bird species.

Gout

The excessive collection of uric acid in the blood and the deposit of urate (see page 123) in tissues and joints is termed gout. The course of the disease is chronic.

The number of gout cases increases in the fall.

Clinical Picture

There are two forms of gout recognized:
(A) Visceral gout is expressed through deposits of urates in the kidney tissue, ureters, pericardium, intestinal tract, air cells, or other organs. It is almost impossible to recognize externally.
(B) Articular gout is more easily diagnosed. The uric acid crystals are deposited under the skin in the area of the joint. You can see roundish, yellow nodules at the joints of the toes and legs and yellowish, crumbly matter in the joints. The wings are usually not affected.
The extremities are often swollen, hot, and painful. In the end stage, the bird can no longer hold onto the perch and sits or lies on the ground.

The sick animals are also indifferent, have watery diarrhea, steadily lose weight, and are weak. Finally, convulsions and sudden death can occur.

Causes

In birds, the uric acid is normally excreted via the kidneys as an end product of protein metabolism. With impairment of the kidneys, this excretion is disturbed. The uric acid level in the blood rises, and urate deposits in the organs and joints results. Gout may also be a consequence of kidney insufficiency.

Also, an obstruction or injury of the ureter leads to pooling of urine, increased uric acid levels, and uric acid deposits.

Infections, poisoning, overdosage of medication, too little water intake, deficiency of vitamin A, and an improper diet favor disease of the kidneys and, thus, often lead to gout.

Excess protein probably contributes to the development of gout and a negative disease course, but it cannot be the cause in itself.

Self-Help

Keep your patient warm and dry. Make a lot of greens and fruit available. In addition, the bird should receive supplementary vitamins A and B in its drinking water or food. Make sure that the bird drinks a lot!

● **Natural Remedies**

Mix Mucosa compositum, Colchicum-Injeel, Traumeel, and Populus compositum in equal parts, and administer three drops of the mixture once a day alternating with one to two drops Solidago compositum.

4

Restructa forte has also been used with very good success. Dissolve one tablet in about one ml of water and administer three to five drops of it to your bird several times a day.

● **Bach Flowers**

Bach Flowers can promote the healing process. Give two drops each of Clematis, Gentian, Larch, and Gorse in 100 ml (3.34 fl oz) of drinking water. You can also add one drop of each from the stock bottle to about 10 ml bottled water, and administer one to four drops (depending on the size of the bird) of this standard dilution to the bird four times a day.

When Should You Go to the Veterinarian?

If you see no improvement after one week and the animal is suffering pain, it is essential that you seek the advice of a veterinarian.

Prevention and Aftercare

Avoid everything that can lead to injury to the kidneys (see Prevention and Aftercare, page 58). Also, keeping the bird in damp, cold quarters can lead to disease.

In the fall months, you should take the precaution of administering to the bird once a week a mixture of Berberis-Homaccord, Cantharis compositum, Carduus compositum, Coenzyme compositum, and Engystol in the drinking water (five drops of the mixture to 10 ml [0.33 fl oz] of drinking water).

In addition, you should always give enough vitamin A and vitamin B12.

Severe gout is even seen in nestlings and juvenile birds. The disease can be prevented if the animals are also offered cow dung. Possibly the protective effect comes from vitamin B12. If you live in a rural area, you may provide your birds with cow pats now and then; however, pet stores have a variety of the appropriate vitamin mixture available.

Species Susceptibility

Gout can appear in all bird species. Budgerigars are affected particularly often.

Diseases of the Male Sex Organs

Diseases of the sex organs most often affect the male in the testes. They lead to decreased reproduction or an impairment of general health. Frequently, there is a transformation in the testes.

Clinical Picture

(A) First and foremost is development of tumors of the testes. Coloration of the cere (e.g., in male budgerigars from blue to brown), easy exhaustion in flight, and diarrhea now and again can be the first symptoms. Later the body swells, dyspnea and paresis occur, and the general state of health is often seriously impaired.

However, a definite external diagnosis is hardly possible.

(B) Although you keep your birds in pairs, they do not reproduce (infertility).

Causes

(A) The causes of tumors of the testes are unclear.

(B) The decrease in reproduction can be a consequence of underdeveloped testes. The circumstances that lead to this developmental defect of the gonads are not known.
Infertility can also be caused by inflammatory changes in the sex organs caused by a variety of pathogens.

Self-Help

Provide a suitable diet (see page 16), adequate vitamin supplements, and correct maintenance (see page 12).

● **Natural Remedies**
(A) A treatment for a testicular tumor can be attempted with a mixture of equal parts of Galium-Heel, Ubichinon compositum, Glyoxal compositum, and Hormeel. Administer three drops of the mixture once daily by mouth or five to eight drops in about 20 to 30 ml (0.7 to 1 fl oz) of drinking water for one week.
Afterwards continue the therapy by administering the medication in the dosages given twice weekly.

Important: With this disease you must exercise much patience and carry out the treatment for a long enough time. In some cases the growth of the tumor can be brought to a halt, or even regression can be achieved (see also Tumors, page 79).

(B) With suspicion of infertility in a male bird, treat the bird for several days with Testis compositum, Hormeel, Carduus compositum, and Coenzyme compositum; give it one drop of each of these substances daily directly in the beak.

● **Bach Flowers**
A misimprinted bird responds well to the Bach Flower Cerato. Administer two drops in 100 ml (3.4 fl oz) of drinking water.

When Should You Go to the Veterinarian?

On suspicion of a tumor you should have the "diagnosis" confirmed.
The veterinarian can also help with sex determination.

What Will the Veterinarian Do?

If you are not sure of the sex of your bird, today the veterinarian is able to have the blood of a number of species tested in a special laboratory to determine whether the animal is a male or a female. With some other species it is still necessary to perform endoscopy (see page 121) for sex determination.

Important: Sex determination by blood test or endoscopy is not done for small bird species to avoid sudden death from shock.

Prevention and Aftercare

With infertility you should always check:
—Are the two mates of the same species?
—Are the mates known to be male and female?
—Are both mates sexually mature?
—Do the two get along, or is there aggression or other dominant behavior?
—Is one of the birds so imprinted on humans that it doesn't recognize one of its own species as a mate?
—Is the cage or aviary arranged so the bird pair feels well and wants to reproduce?
—Is the diet correct, and does it contain enough vitamins and minerals?

4

If tumors actually regress, the treatment should be continued for one month longer.

Species Susceptibility

Tumor formation in the testicles is very common in budgerigars. They occur at all age levels of animal.

Diseases of the Female Sex Organs

Disorders in egg development occur relatively often.

Clinical Picture

(A) The female lays eggs that are misshapen, are too large, or have too soft a shell, (wind eggs). (see page 123).

Important: Such eggs can lead to egg binding (see page 100). In this case, the need for help is urgent!

(B) The bird lays no eggs and will not breed.
(C) Her body swells considerably, she has dyspnea and diarrhea, she vomits, and the fecal masses are enlarged. Eventually, she becomes unsteady on her legs. In some, the nasal cere is discolored. The general state of health can be markedly deteriorated.
Some ailing birds keep straining even though there is no egg in the oviduct.
In serious cases, sudden death can even occur, at first glance, apparently inexplicably.

Causes

(A) Such egg anomalies are often a symptom of inflammatory processes in the area of the genital organs. When the shell is too soft or incomplete, this can also indicate exhaustion of the bird through overproduction. The calcium reserves are used up.
(B) As of today there is little understanding of the reasons for reproductive disorders in female birds. The possible causes of infertility in males should also be checked in females (see Prevention and Aftercare, page 61).
(C) The swelling can indicate tumors and cysts of the ovaries. But an oviduct that is very enlarged and filled with whitish mucus or pus and possibly egg matter (salpingitis) can also produce these symptoms.
Causes can also be an inflammation of the abdominal cavity (egg peritonitis) produced by egg yolk that has entered the abdominal cavity through tears in the oviduct.

Self-Help

(A) Check the diet and living conditions for sufficient provision of vitamins and minerals, correct feed (see page 16), enough warmth, and proper hygiene.
Move the bird to other surroundings so it stops developing eggs. Reduce the light for this.

Important: Inadequate hygiene can permit the spread of infectious diseases that involve the genital organs.

(B) Pay attention to health, vitamin-rich food, and correct and warm living conditions. In addition you should provide the right sort of lighting. In decreased light, as in winter, eggs do not mature.

Check to see whether the nesting conditions you are providing are correct for the species. For reproductive impairment, see also Prevention and Aftercare, page 61.

● **Natural Remedies**

(A) Give the bird one drop each of Echinacea compositum, Mucosa compositum, and Pulsatilla compositum daily in the beak.

(B) You can promote readiness to breed with Ovarium compositum, Carduus compositum, and Coenzyme compositum—one drop per day in the beak.

(C) Try therapy with Galium-Heel, Glyoxal compositum, Ubichinon compositum, Ovarium compositum, and Lachesis compositum. Mix these medicines in equal parts and administer two to three drops of the mixture per day directly in the beak.

● **Bach Flowers**

With the administration of two drops Olive essence to 100 ml (3.4 fl oz) of drinking water, you can help a bird that is exhausted by overproduction to regain its strength.

When Should You Go to the Veterinarian?

(A) If your bird repeatedly lays deformed or soft-shelled eggs, you should show it to the veterinarian soon because of the danger of egg binding.

(B) If you are not quite sure whether the affected bird is a female, you must consult a veterinarian for sex determination by blood test or endoscopy (see page 121).

(C) You should always have a veterinarian look immediately at a bird with a swollen body to establish the cause. The chances of cure are not good. In some cases an operation may be appropriate.

Prevention and Aftercare

Provide an appropriate, high-value diet (see page 16) and living conditions (see page 12), as well as strict hygiene.

Avoid letting the bird get fat. During egg maturation and laying protect your bird from any stress, increased excitement, and risk of injury. Observe the laying hen very carefully.

Species Susceptibility

Budgerigars and other parrots suffer more from tumor formation in the ovaries than other birds.

Prolapsed Oviduct

4

Clinical Picture

A piece of the oviduct is extruded from the cloaca. Sometimes it contains a deformed egg. The bird is exhausted from straining a long time.

Causes

Usually an episode of egg binding (see page 100) has preceded it.

The constant straining in connection with a salpingitis (see page 62) can also produce an oviduct prolapse.

Self-Help

Rinse the prolapsed oviduct with a warm solution of table salt and water in order to remove any sand, seed, and fecal matter that may be clinging to it. If there is an egg in it, carefully press it along and completely remove all the remains. Daub the prolapsed piece and the cloaca with Traumeel-ointment, and carefully press the oviduct back in.

It is essential that you consult a veterinarian to confirm the diagnosis.

● Natural Remedies
Give one drop each of Ovarium compositum and Traumeel per day for one week. To strengthen the exhausted animal, it is also recommended to give one drop each of Carduus compositum and Coenzyme compositum per day.

● Bach Flowers
In addition, it is helpful to give two drops of Rescue Remedy in 50 ml (1.69 fl oz) of drinking water.

What Will the Veterinarian Do?

If the prolapse has existed for a while and the oviduct is either dried out or even necrotic, the section may have to be amputated by a veterinarian.

Prevention and Aftercare

Warmth is an important remedy.

After an oviduct prolapse you should not use the hen for breeding anymore. It could easily lead to a recurrence of the problem.

Inadequate Brood Care

Clinical Picture

One or both mates take no interest in matters of the eggs and the young as is appropriate to their species. They give an impression of being uncertain or put upon too much. The stress of brooding is just too much for some birds. They abandon the nest or even eat their own eggs or young.

Causes

The causes are largely undetermined. Neurotic behavior is suggested. Possibly other birds in the same aviary are disturbing the nesting pair. Also, overbreeding may play a role.

Self-Help

Provide for an adequately warm, quiet environment for the nesting pair.

Make sure the diet is correct for the species (see page 20).

If nesting is taking place in an aviary, you should make sure that no rats, cats, or humans disturb the nesting pair. If there are other birds in the aviary, you should put these in another cage during the brooding period.

● Bach Flowers
If the parents aren't paying enough attention to the nest or the young or they even try to eat them, they need the Bach Flower Chestnut Bud. You can promote the bird's natural instincts for brood care by giving it Scleranthus before the start of the nesting season. Walnut will help bird mothers and fathers that are brooding for the first time cope better with the stress of brooding.

Give two drops of each Bach Flower in 100 ml (3.4 fl oz) of drinking water during the entire brooding and raising period to the birds.

Diseases of the Feathers and Skin

The skin of the bird is characteristically thinner and more sensitive than that of other animals. In many places, such as the wing tips and the legs, it is very close to the skeleton. Only in a comparatively few areas is there muscle between the skin and the skeleton.

The skin consists of the upper layer (epidermis), the connective tissue true skin (corium or dermis), and the bottom layer (subcutis). The difference of the skin in feathered and unfeathered areas like the legs and toes is clearly visible. Here the epidermis is characteristically thicker than on body surfaces protected by the plumage. The feathers are formed in the epidermis and the dermis.

The development of the feathers and the structure of the entire plumage is altogether fascinating. The first sign that a feather is developing is a disk-shaped swelling of the epidermis. Then a pointed elevation forms that proceeds to sink into the skin. The feather follicle is developing. It consists of epidermis and dermis. In the pith of the developing feather is an artery and a vein; in the course of the maturation of the feather the pith diminishes. When an immature feather is torn out, considerable bleeding occurs. But bleeding also occurs with the pulling out of mature feathers, because the feather's connection with the follicle and the very highly vascularized so-called dermal papilla is ruptured.

For the structure of the feather and the different types of feathers, see the inside front cover and definitions on pages 122–123.

Most bird species change their plumage at least once a year; this process is called molting (see page 75).

The alert animal owner usually can easily recognize diseases of the skin and disorders of feather growth and treat them.

For feather plucking see page 91.

Skin Wounds

Clinical Picture

Sticky, sometimes blood-smeared feathers are signs of injury to the skin.

Important: The animal should be examined thoroughly at once, for even the slightest blood loss can lead to death. On the other hand, wound infections rarely occur in birds.

Causes

Wounds can be caused in groups of captive birds through fights for dominance or other aggressive behavior.

Inappropriate cage equipment, such as toys, cats, or accidents during free flight are also possible causes.

Crash landings lead to injuries of the breastbone.

Self-Help

As a rule, birds have good wound recovery. Paint tears and cuts at once with a cotton swab dipped in ferric chloride to stop the bleeding. You can also use styptic cotton.

For follow-up treatment use Arnica tincture or Traumeel-ointment.

● Natural Remedies

Give the bird two drops of Traumeel twice a day directly in the beak to hasten wound healing and protect it from infection. The treatment should be repeated for the next two days.

When Should You Go to the Veterinarian?

Large wounds must be sutured by a veterinarian so no bare spots will be left. If bone tissue is exposed, surgical procedures are required.

Prevention and Aftercare

When you introduce new birds you should observe them for a while to see how they get along. It is always better if the birds can get to know each other for a time at a distance in separate cages. Even among groups of birds that are considered quite peaceful, like the waxbills, there are some that are markedly quarrelsome.

Make sure that the cages or aviaries don't have any sharp edges or points on which your birds can injure themselves.

Cats should not be allowed to get near cages without supervision, even if not all cats try to catch birds in cages!

Before you let your bird fly free, you should check the surroundings very carefully for the potential dangers of injury.

Red Chicken Mites

This parasite rarely appears in house birds that are kept alone. On the other hand, it is very common in aviaries.

Mites are members of the spider family. They have eight legs and are very active. The females deposit their eggs in chinks.

Clinical Picture

The birds are very restless at night. In advanced stages, the skin is strikingly pale, the animals waste away, and they can even die. It is primarily nestlings that are suddenly found dead. Affected birds fidget nervously with their feathers.

If you cover the cage or aviary with a white cloth at night, on close examination the next morning there will probably be countless dark-red or black moving dots, which under the magnifying glass show themselves to be mites.

Important: While an attack of red chicken mites manifests itself in restlessness at night, birds that are suffering from the northern fowl mite (see page 69) are restless during the day.

Causes

The birds are attacked by the red chicken mite. This nocturnally active parasite, about 0.6 mm in size, is especially prevalent in warm summers. It multiplies extremely fast.

In the dark it sucks on the bird's blood. At daybreak it hides in the nesting material and in the chinks and cracks of the cage or the surrounding area. Sometimes you even find individual mites under the wings or in bends of the elbow and shoulder.

Self-Help

Clean the cage or aviary and every object as thoroughly as possible with hot water, to which you have added *baking soda*. Pay special attention to all wooden parts, cracks, and crevices. Also inspect the area around the cage. Cracks in walls, curtains, and so on offer good hiding places for mites.

Completely change all floor coverings and nesting material whenever there is an attack.

Finally, spray everything very intensively with an organic, nontoxic mite spray. This material is completely nontoxic and, therefore, outstandingly suitable for use on the bird itself and its surroundings. The birds need not be taken out of the aviary during the spray treatment. The mite spray does not work like regular insecticide with toxic materials but by mechanically obstructing the airways of this tiny parasite. It is not harmful for birds but, on the contrary, has a grooming effect. The birds must also be sprayed very thoroughly, especially under the wings.

These measures should be carried out daily for ten days and then once weekly for at least three weeks to be certain that all offspring of the mites have been caught.

Important: Never spray a clutch of eggs with the material. It will close the pores of the egg, and the bird embryos will suffocate.

For regeneration after a loss of blood, you should give your bird 1 ml Plastisan in 50 ml (1.69 fl oz) of drinking water every fourteen days.

● **Natural Remedies**

For support, give the bird Carduus compositum and Coenzyme compositum, directly if possible (two drops of each every two days for one week) or in the drinking water (five drops each in 10 ml [0.34 fl oz]).

When Should You Go to the Veterinarian?

Should your early treatment still show no adequate effect despite all measures, you must have the veterinarian give you an insecticide suitable for use on a bird.

Important: Many of the commercially available pesticides are highly toxic to sensitive bird species. Don't let yourself be misled into using them without having a discussion with a veterinarian. It will do you no good if the parasites are exterminated faster but the birds sustain severe liver damage from it or die.

Prevention and Aftercare

Inspect the cage, aviary, nests, and all items of equipment and toys for mites regularly. After the young are raised, change the nesting material. Observe whether your birds are restless at night. Now and then (even after treatment) perform the test with the white cloth (see page 66).

Burrowing Mites

Infestation with burrowing mites is also known as scaly face and scaly legs.

Clinical Picture

Gray-white, porous, spongelike growths extend around the base of the beak, nose, and eye re-

5

gions. Notable are countless tiny bore holes that have given the disease the name of beak sponge.

Also, the legs, feet, and cloaca can be covered with chalky, porous masses (scaly leg). In well-advanced, severe cases these can extend to crusty deposits over the entire body.

They can be easily removed.

The skin is swollen and the tunnels chewed by the mites (the little bore holes) are clearly recognizable.

The birds twitch and shudder, tear out their feathers, and injure themselves with their own beaks. The feathers are usually missing on affected areas of the skin.

Often the beak is left deformed.

Causes

The cause of the growths on the beak is the burrowing mite *Knemidokoptes pilae.*

So-called scaly leg is caused by a related species, the scaly-leg mite *K. mutans.*

The approximately 0.4 mm large mite eats tunnels into the epidermis and attacks the feather follicle. It passes its entire life cycle on the bird host. These burrowing mites are transmitted to the nestlings by the adult birds.

As a rule, the disease breaks out because of diminished resistance or other infections. Also, bad maintenance conditions can be responsible for it.

Self-Help

The excrescences or abnormal growths on the skin are softened with glycerine and carefully removed. You should follow-up with a thorough daily spraying with an organic, nontoxic mite spray for one to two weeks. The substance can also be painted on. Completely wetting the af-

fected areas is important. For supplementary support, add a good multivitamin preparation containing adequate vitamin A to the drinking water.

● **Natural Remedies**

To strengthen resistance, mix Carduus compositum, Coenzyme compositum, and Cutis compositum in equal parts, and give the bird two drops daily by mouth for five days. Repeat this treatment once again after one week and after another two weeks.

● **Bach Flowers**

Administer one drop of Crab Apple daily in the drinking water.

When Should You Go to the Veterinarian?

If the general state of health is impaired and your treatment shows no improvement within three to four days, you should take your bird to a veterinarian.

Prevention and Aftercare

Provide correct maintenance and diet (see pages 12 and 16). Also, make sure you give the bird enough greens, carrots, and fruit. Spray the bird preventively with an organic, nontoxic mite spray once a week.

Species Susceptibility

Scaly face is found primarily in budgerigars and (rarely) in other parrots.

Young birds are affected often.

Songbirds like canaries and waxbills commonly suffer from scaly leg.

Other Ectoparasites

Other ectoparasites of the skin and feathers are skin mites, feather mites, quill mites, bird lice, lice, louse flies, and ticks.

Birds kept in the house come into contact with such parasites much more rarely than animals that live in outdoor aviaries or whose cages are placed outside. (But that should not be taken as an argument against keeping birds outdoors!)

Birds at risk should regularly be observed closely and at the slightest suspicion be thoroughly examined for parasites. Mites can transmit infectious diseases.

Clinical Picture and Causes

Most of these parasites are about 0.6 mm and can be recognized with the naked eye when you inspect the feathers and the skin, especially under the wings. With almost all of them, the feathers look pulled apart or unkempt, the birds are restless, they groom themselves excessively, and they even pull their feathers out.

(A) Besides the red chicken mite (see page 66), other kinds of *skin mites* occur, especially in many songbirds. The plumage is picked at, the skin is inflamed, and the birds are restless throughout the day. Some mites, like the *northern chicken mite*, cause anemia. Some mites bury themselves under small, white webs.

To differentiate between red and northern chicken mites, see page 66.

(B) *Feather mites* parasitize the shafts of the feathers of the wing and tail. The females lay their eggs on the shafts. The nymphs hatch and eat there.

(C) *Quill mites or feather follicle mites* nest in the quills of the wing and tail feathers, which produces inflammation. The feathers fall out, break off, or remain undeveloped. The quill is filled with a powdery matter.

Sometimes tumors or cystlike formations appear in the skin, in which, after being opened, the mites and parts of destroyed feathers are found.

(D) *Bird lice* are the most commonly seen parasites of the feather. In general, they get their nourishment from the skin scales and from the keratin of the feathers. Some species also ingest blood. In severe attacks, the feathers are pulled out and gnawed.

Bird lice cause severe itching, probably through the irritation of the sensitive filoplume (see page 122). The birds are very restless. On close examination, the brown, 1 to 3 mm long bird lice and their ashy gray egg deposits can be seen on the feathers.

(E) *Louse flies* and *lice* can usually be kept in check by the bird itself through its diligent feather grooming. But they irritate the bird severely and can transmit other diseases. Animals already weakened can be particularly endangered by the bloodsucking louse flies.

(F) *Ticks* rarely turn up on birds in captivity, but through the toxin that they inject into the bloodstream with their bite, they can cause fatal hematomas in smaller species.

The ornamental birds can catch the parasites through contact with wild birds or a sojourn out of doors. New acquisitions can already have been infected by them.

Self-Help

If you are keeping several birds and they don't all show the same symptoms, you should immedi-

ately separate the affected birds from one another. Inspect the birds carefully. You can take
off the larger parasites; carefully pull out ticks.
Spray the plumage daily for three weeks with an
organic, nontoxic mite spray. Also, thoroughly
clean the aviary or cage, including all the objects
in it, and change the floor covering and nesting
materials. Furthermore, you should thoroughly
spray the aviary.

To build it up, give the bird 1 ml Plastisan in
50 ml of drinking water for fourteen days.

Important: Larger parasites like ticks should be
removed by hand, because the mite spray
isn't effective enough on them.

● **Natural Remedies**

Give the affected birds one drop each of Carduus compositum, Coenzyme compositum, and
Cutis compositum every three days by mouth.

When Should You Go to the Veterinarian?

If in spite of your treatment the parasites are
not entirely banished, you should go to a veterinarian.

What Will the Veterinarian Do?

The veterinarian will give you a safe insecticide
that is tolerated by birds. If you have found
feather follicle cysts, he will clean them out.

Prevention and Aftercare

Inspect your bird regularly and thoroughly. If
you have acquired a new bird, you should keep it
quarantined for at least two weeks after first examining it very thoroughly.

As a preventive measure, spray your bird and
its living quarters with an organic, nontoxic mite
spray regular intervals.

Always be careful about hygiene. Mites can
also infect humans.

Eczema

Many causes of skin disease are very difficult for
the average person to diagnose. This is the case
with eczema.

The head, neck, and rump of the bird are affected.

Clinical Picture

The skin is often somewhat thickened; affected
places are not clearly defined. The surfaces of
the skin areas are often moist and raspberry colored. Deposits or crusts can appear. Local loss of
feathers is observed. The bird nibbles or
scratches at the itching places.

Sometimes slight diarrhea occurs at the same
time.

Causes

Metabolic derangements or disorders of the liver
or kidneys are often the causes of eczemas. The
necessary urinary substances and other metabolic
products are then excreted through the skin.

Unclean drinking water, dirty food dishes,
spoiled food, and the wrong food composition
can trigger eczema.

Self-Help

Add a vitamin A supplement to the drinking
water. Local treatment of the ailing skin is not

advisable, because the spots may only be more irritated by it.

Important: Never use skin salves or lotions that have been prescribed for you or another person for eczema or similar conditions. Many of these treatments for humans contain additives that are extremely toxic to birds.

● **Natural Remedies**

As a rule, eczema heals very rapidly with Traumeel, Cutis compositum, Carduus compositum, and Coenzyme compositum; give one drop of each daily by mouth for two weeks.

If there is no improvement after three to four days, change to Psorinoheel, Carduus compositum, and Coenzyme compositum in the same dosage.

If the skin is covered with small, hard blisters (vesicles), you should use Bufo-Injeel. Use one drop daily for two weeks.

● **Bach Flowers**

In addition, you should add one drop of Crab Apple daily to the drinking water.

When Should You Go to the Veterinarian?

If despite treatment the signs do not disappear after one week, a veterinarian must be consulted. However, you should go to the veterinarian at once if the general condition of health is poor.

Prevention and Aftercare

A proper diet with sufficient vitamin A is an essential contribution to prevention. The food and the food dishes must be in faultless condition.

Also, protect your bird from ingesting toxic substances.

Fungus Diseases of the Skin

If you find a skin change in your bird that resists all attempts at treatment, you should consider the possibility of a fungus infection, especially if disorders of the airway develop.

Clinical Picture

Round, demarcated scaly areas are visible on the skin, and the changes appear two-dimensional. The surrounding area is intact. The border area appears brownish white, while the center is gray white.

However, the skin lesions can also take other forms, depending on the species of fungus involved.

Causes

These skin lesions can be caused by fungi or yeasts. There are more than ten different species involved, with varying symptoms.

Fungi have the best chances to colonize when the bird's resistance is already weakened or the skin has already been damaged, perhaps by an attack of mites.

Important: Should symptoms of airway distress occur at the same time, it is cause for the greatest alarm. Fungi can also attack the respiratory organs, and that is life threatening.

Self-Help

Daub the affected skin areas with a cotton swab with Iodoglycerine 1:5 daily for two weeks.

5

Add supplementary vitamins, particularly vitamin A, to the drinking water.

● Natural Remedies

Support healing with Sulfur-Injeel forte and Sodium-Homaccord. Administer both medicines alternately for one week one drop daily directly in the beak—sulfur one day, sodium the next. Finally, on the seventh and the fourteenth day after this treatment, give both preparations once more.

When Should You Go to the Veterinarian?

If the bird's general state of health is bad, if you suspect an ailment of the airway at the same time, or if the skin lesions do not get better within a few days despite treatment, you should consult a veterinarian.

Prevention and Aftercare

Check to be sure that living conditions and diet are optimal and make sure that you are providing adequate vitamin A.

Honeycomb Ringworm

This disease is also known as favus.

Clinical Picture

On the upper head, especially around the quills, appears a white, moldlike deposit in the form of spots and scabs. The face is also often affected.

The process extends into the feather follicle and leads to feather dropping. The bird loses weight.

Causes

Honeycomb ringworm is caused by the fungus *Trichophyton*. The fungus is transmitted by direct contact and through the air.

Self-Help

Isolate the affected bird. The cage and its furnishings should be washed thoroughly.

Treat the affected places thoroughly every day with Iodoglycerine 1:5. Provide adequate vitamin supplements and optimal living conditions. In addition, add Plastisan to the drinking water for two weeks (1 ml to 100 ml [3.4 fl oz] of water).

● Natural Remedies

In addition, oral administration of Carduus compositum, Coenzyme compositum, and Cutis compositum is necessary. Mix the medicines in equal parts and give two to three drops of the mixture per day for two to three weeks.

When Should You Go to the Veterinarian?

If there is no improvement after five days, you should go to a veterinarian.

Prevention and Aftercare

Food and living conditions that are not right for the species can weaken your bird's powers of resistance, and fungus and favus will have an easy time of it. Make sure you offer optimal living conditions (see page 12).

Species Susceptibility

Besides being seen in chickens, the disease has been observed in canaries and some other ornamental birds.

Warts

Clinical Picture

Raised, demarcated, plate-shaped or pointed skin growths with rough, dry surfaces are seen. They are often on eyelids and in the corners of the beak but are also found in the cloaca.

Causes

These skin lesions are probably warts or benign tumors that are produced by the papillomavirus. The disease occurs under stress or after small skin wounds.

Self-Help

Important: Don't under any circumstances attempt to remove these growths. This can cause severe bleeding with a great loss of blood that can be fatal

● **Natural Remedies**
Administer one to two drops Thuja-Injeel daily by mouth, for an extended period, if possible. This produces drying of the warts. The skin growths will then fall off.

When Should You Go to the Veterinarian?

If no change occurs after two weeks, a veterinarian must be consulted.

What Will the Veterinarian Do?

The veterinarian can remove the growths with a laser or electrocautery.

Prevention and Aftercare

Avoid stressful situations for your bird.

Species Susceptibility

These skin growths are found relatively often in gray parrots, aras, and amazons.

Xanthematosis

Clinical Picture

Locally the skin has tumorlike lesions, is extremely swollen, is colored ochre-yellow, is of generally fragile condition, and is strongly vascularized. The birds often pick these skin lesions (xanthomas) open, resulting in life-threatening hemorrhages.

Causes

The causes of these tumerous skin lesions have not been clearly explained.

Self-Help

Stop hemorrhages immediately with a cotton swab dipped in ferric chloride (see page 96). Self-help procedures with this disease can only be accompanying therapy to the veterinary treatment.

● **Natural Remedies**
Ancillary therapy can be tried with Lymphomyosot and Sulfur-Injeel. Mix the medicines in equal parts, and give two drops per day by mouth.

5

When Should You Go to the Veterinarian?

These skin lesions should be shown to a veterinarian immediately. Surgical removal may be possible.

Species Susceptibility

This condition is found more often in budgerigars and cockatoos.

Pox

Many bird species can be infected with pox. Among them are canaries, other finches, and parrots. Among the parrots alone there are three different kinds of the virus—for lovebirds, amazons, and budgerigars.

Many infected birds die, but with timely treatment there is a chance of survival.

The pox virus infection occurs in two different forms depending on whether the skin or the mucous membranes are affected.

The disease breaks out primarily in the fall.

Clinical Picture

One of the symptoms of pox is severe lesions of the skin and mucous membranes.

Papules appear in the cutaneous form, flat at first, later raised, usually around the eye at first, on the nose, at the corners of the beak, and on the legs. The pox can spread to scabby excrescences. If no further infection occurs, the pox can heal in several weeks.

Important: Pox should always be considered when there are wounds that do not heal quickly.

In the mucous membrane form, or diphtheria, the mucous membranes of the beak cavity and the jaws are severely inflamed and are covered with thick, whitish false membrane that quickly spreads. If the lungs are also affected, the birds are seen gasping for air by breathing through their open beaks. In these cases the birds have trouble swallowing and suffer from severe dyspnea that is frequently associated with red and swollen eyes and with nasal discharge.

There is little chance of recovery from this form of the disease.

Causes

The disease is caused by the poxvirus. The infection occurs by direct contact through contaminated drinking water, food, dust, or bloodsucking parasites and insects like mites, louse flies, or gnats.

The period of contagion can run from four to sixteen days.

Self-Help

Warmth and a high dosage of vitamin A are important in order to increase the animal's resistance. If you keep several birds, you must isolate the affected one at once, because the disease is highly contagious.

Important: With the mucous membrane form of this disease, you must see to it that the bird takes in enough water and (liquid) food.

● **Natural Remedies**
In conjunction with the veterinarian's treatment, you can give the bird one drop each of Engystol and Mucosa compositum daily by mouth for two to three weeks.

● **Bach Flowers**

To increase the birds powers of resistance, administer one drop Crab Apple and Centaury daily in the drinking water.

When Should You Go to the Veterinarian?

All pox-infected birds should be seen by a veterinarian.

What Will the Veterinarian Do?

The veterinarian can sometimes save canaries and other finches with a vaccine injection. For parrots, however, a vaccine is currently not available.

Prevention and Aftercare

Larger groups of canaries and finches should be vaccinated every year in June or July. Diseased birds must remain in quarantine for at least six weeks after cure.

Molting Disorders

Molting is not a disease but a natural process in the life of a bird where the old feathers are replaced by newly grown ones. This is very practical, because the plumage has probably worn out or has been damaged over time. In most bird species, molting takes place once a year, usually after the breeding season in late summer or early fall. There are also some species that molt two or three times a year, and others, like some of the parrots, that keep changing a portion of their feathers throughout the entire year. On the other hand, some large parrots need up to two years for a complete molting cycle. At the beginning of the mating season, some species change to a special breeding plumage.

Influences on molting include in the changes in length of the day, the temperature, and thyroid and sex homones. Stress can also influence the course of the feather change.

The bird never loses all its feathers at the same time during molting. The wing and tail feathers are gradually exchanged on both sides over a period of two to three weeks. The other feathers are also continuously replaced. In a normal molt, there are no bare places showing, and the bird remains able to fly. But there can be uncertainties in flying, with increased risks of accidents.

The change of feathers takes place without bleeding, but the newly developed feathers are still provided with arteries and veins in the quill until, as the feather matures, the pith redevelops. Gradually during growth, the feather sheath ruptures and releases the barbs and the barbules.

If the feathers are destroyed or pulled out outside the normal molting season, the bird can replace them. However, the prerequisite is that the entire feather, including the quill, must be removed first. The shaft must not be broken and remain in the follicle.

Normally, molting has hardly any effect on the general state of health of a healthy bird. However, it does make heavy demands on the body, and the bird usually exhibits an increased need for sleep. The development of the new feathers leads to a temporary demineralization of the bones and to an increased risk of bone fracture.

However, many disorders can occur in connection with molting.

Clinical Picture

(A) The feathers fall out, but don't grow back or grow back incompletely or malformed (stuck-in-the-molt-syndrome). The deformed feather

5

vanes sometimes stick halfway in their sheaths and open pencil shaped on top. Bald spots occur.

Eventually the general health condition declines. Some birds try to pick at the undeveloped feathers thereby causing bleeding and feather quills to be engorged with blood.

(B) The new feathers exhibit abnormal colors. Previously gray feathers are reddish or pink now, and instead of dark brown or green the feathers are black now.

Bare spots occur, primarily on the abdomen, and eczema appears. Sometimes the feather growth is delayed.

In addition, the tips of the feathers or parts of the plumage become black.

(C) The bird loses feathers symmetrically on both sides. There may also be growth disorders of feathers, feather anomalies, and black tips. Sometimes the entire plumage becomes downlike.

(D) Feathers fall out, and the plumage is dull. The general condition is undisturbed.

(E) Feathers from all over the body fall out or break off. The plumage color fades, and at the same time, the beak becomes soft and deformed.

Important: In contrast to feather plucking (see page 91), here the head is also involved!

Causes

(A) Frequently, the cause of this should be sought in a deficiency of vitamins, minerals, and amino acids. Because molting usually begins after the also stressful mating season, the bird can quickly develop a deficiency. Especially at risk are birds that have not been fed a proper diet, like many large parakeets and parrots that in their natural habitats also eat animal protein.

Also faulty maintenance, such as too small a cage, should be considered as a cause.

(B) Behind this plumage discoloration lie other primary diseases, such as liver damage. This can be caused by moldy food, for example, or too many fatty seeds. For instance, *Amadina* parrots get liver disease from hemp almost without exception.

Also inadequate exercise and lack of direct sunlight can produce alterations in the plumage color.

Kidney disease is also accompanied by a loss of feathers, deformities, and eczema, although usually without the typical discoloration.

(C) Probably hypothroidism is responsible for these symptoms.

(D) Disturbances of sexual hormone balance often result in these plumage changes. Usually older birds are affected.

(E) The cause of this problem is usually the psittacine beak and feather disease (PBFD). This is a viral disease that is found in more than thirty-five parrot species. Many birds are carriers of the virus without becoming ill. Only when the immune system is weakened, does the disease break out. But then the outcome is usually fatal.

Only among lovebirds has survival of PBFD and normal refeathering several months after total baldness been reported.

Self-Help

(A) Offer as complete and varied a diet as possible. For several weeks give additional vitamins, minerals, and amino acids. Make sure that the cage is large enough! You can stop bleeding with ferric chloride. If necessary, remove the bleeding quill and press the follicle together.

You should enrich the drinking water for the next three weeks with 1 ml Plastisan per 50 ml of water.

(B) Check the feed to be sure it isn't spoiled or moldy. Remove the peanuts because they are almost always moldy.

Remove hemp and other very fatty seeds from the menu. Feed plenty of vitamins, greens, and fruit.

(See also Liver Diseases, page 55, and Kidney Inflammation, page 57.)

(C) The bird should receive vitamins and additional iodine via the drinking water (one drop to 25 ml water). Provide for sufficient exercise.

(D) Give vitamin supplements and make sure that the bird receives enough light and sun.

(E) The chance of cure among species other than the lovebirds is poor. If you want to try, provide optimal living conditions with fresh air and very nutritious food high in multivitamin supplements. Inspect the beak and claws for softening. Eventually, you must offer liquid food.

● Natural Remedies

(A) Give one drop each of Carduus compositum, Coenzyme compositum, and Cutis compositum daily by beak for fourteen days in conjunction with the measures given above. This usually brings about healing.

For molting problems, an alternative therapy with Sodium muriaticum d6X, Calcium fluoratum 12X, and Silicea 12X can be initiated. Give one drop of each daily.

(B) Try treatment with one drop each of Carduus compositum, Coenzyme compositum, Cutis compositum, and Cerebrum compositum every two days for four weeks.

(C) For support administer two drops Thyreoidea compositum three times per week; on the in-

tervening days give the bird one drop of Calcium iodatum 12X.

(D) At the beginning of the molt, give the bird one drop each of Ovarium compositum, Hormeel, and Cerebrum compositum daily for one week. During the following two weeks, administer a combination Carduus compositum, Coenzyme compositum, and Cutis compositum. You can administer one drop of each remedy directly into the beak, or you can prepare a mixture of equal parts and add 1 ml of the mixture to the drinking water.

(E) Try a cure with Engystol and Coenzyme compositum. Give one drop of each daily in the first week, every two days in the second week, and then once a week.

● Bach Flowers

(E) Olive, Hornbeam, Agrimony, and Wild Rose are effective in strengthening the bird. Give one drop of each in about 30 to 50 ml of drinking water for several weeks.

In all other cases of feather development disorders, itching, and feather plucking, you should give supplements of the Bach Flower essences Agrimony, Hornbeam, Impatiens, Crab Apple, and Mustard (one drop of each in the drinking water).

When Should You Go to the Veterinarian?

If your bird does not respond to treatment within a few days, you should consult a veterinarian.

Prevention and Aftercare

Provide humidity and warmth. These promote molting. Budgerigars, for example, need a relative humidity of sixty percent for a good molting cycle.

5

It is very important, even during the breeding season or for birds that are not breeding at the beginning of molting, to provide optimal conditions to exclude the possibility of deficiency diseases. You should provide a complete, varied diet, additional vitamins and minerals, and enough light and exercise.

Species Susceptibility

Basically, molting problems occur in all species. The dangerous feather-loss syndrome (PBFD, see page 123) is only reported in parrots.

Terror Molting

Clinical Picture

In a moment of great anxiety or terror, the bird suddenly loses many feathers, among them most often the large tail feathers.

Causes

This sudden shedding of large quantities of feathers in stress situations is thought to be a defense mechanism against natural enemies that can save the endangered bird's life. The feathers on the wings are not affected, so the bird retains its ability to fly. The feathers will grow back soon.

Self-Help

● **Bach Flowers**
Rock Rose, Mimulus, and Beech as well as Rescue Remedy drops, can help the bird overcome its anxiety. Give it one drop of each every day in the drinking water.

French Molting

This disease is a problem in many a brood. It is also called runner or hopper disease.

Clinical Picture

The young birds suddenly lose their tail and wing feathers shortly before they leave the nest. They become unable to fly and are aptly termed "runner," or "hopper." Their general health condition is unaffected. Sometimes the feathers grow back; in other cases the birds remain unable to fly all their lives.

Causes

The causes are not understood. External or diet-related influences, genetic factors, viruses, or a combination of all of them are possible causes.

Self-Help

You can only do something preventively.

Prevention and Aftercare

Be sure to provide a balanced, varied diet (see page 16) and optimal living conditions (see page 12). Do not allow your birds to breed more than twice a year.

Species Susceptibility

Young budgerigars and other small parakeet species can develop into runners.

Preen Gland Disease

The preen (uropygeal) gland is located just in front of the base of the tail feathers. It secretes an oily substance with which the bird grooms its feathers.

Clinical Picture

The gland is considerably swollen, the bird's general health condition is affected. The feathers become dull and sticky and are no longer water repellent.

Some birds pick at the enlarged and inflamed preen gland and cause wounds and bleeding.

Causes

A blockage of the secretory duct causes pooling of secretions and subsequently the inflammation of the preen gland.

Self-Help

Try, with careful massage, to completely empty the gland.

For grooming the plumage, you can spray the bird daily with an organic, nontoxic mite spray.

● **Natural Remedies**

Rub Traumeel ointment into the gland area daily for two weeks.

At the same time give the bird one to two drops of Traumeel and Paeonia officinalis-Injeel forte orally for one week.

When Should You Go to the Veterinarian?

If you are unable to empty the preen gland completely, have this done by a veterinarian, possibly with a surgical procedure.

Prevention and Aftercare

Check to be sure the maintenance conditions and diet are correct for your bird.

Tumors

Development of tumors on the skin, the inner organs, the extremities, and in the head region are found relatively commonly. A distinction must be made between benign and malignant neoplasms.

With benign tumors the general state of health is not particularly affected.

With malignant tumors the general state of health is impaired. They often display a rapid increase in size and do not remain contained at the place of origin but spread into the surrounding tissue and form daughter tumors in other organs.

Clinical Picture

(A) Lipomas are often found in the chest region and more rarely in other regions of the body. These are usually movable, well-defined, soft tumors that grow slowly but achieve considerable size and can handicap the animal. Often the affected birds are clumsy and short of breath.

Sometimes the birds pick at these growths, which can lead to severe bleeding.

Lipomas are benign tumors, as are xanthomas (see page 73), warts, and feather follicle cysts. Most other neoplasms of the skin must be classified as malignant.

(B) Birds may exhibit breathing difficulties, diarrhea, and apathy. Often the body is swollen.

5

In affected male budgerigars, typically the color of the nasal cere changes from blue to dark brown. On palpation the abdomen feels very full.

Causes

(A) The development of lipomas may be due to hormonal disorders, excess weight, insufficient exercise, and mechanical irritation. These fatty tumors often develop from fat deposits that are not worked off.

Wild birds naturally build up fat deposits as provisions for long flights. Our caged birds also build up these reserves, but they don't use them.

(B) The weight indicates an internal tumor. Most tumors of the inner organs are malignant. Tumors of the liver, kidneys, thyroid, ovaries, or testes occur relatively frequently.

The presence of an internal tumor cannot be diagnosed with one hundred percent certainty in a living bird and remains only a suspicion for the time being.

Why tumors develop is unclear.

Self-Help

(A) Decrease the amount of food and use a diet feed that is as rich in vitamins and as varied as possible (see Liver Diet, page 114).

Allow the bird free flight and check to be sure the cage is big enough.

(B) Provide optimal living conditions (see page 12) and supplement the feed with vitamins (see page 16).

● Natural Remedies

(A) Give the bird one drop each of Carduus compositum and Coenzyme compositum daily over an extended period.

You can also administer one drop each of Glyoxal compositum and Ubichinon compositum daily.

If the lipoma continues to enlarge, you should also administer one drop each of Galium-Heel and Lymphomyosot.

(B) With some malignant tumors, the chances for healing with homeopathic therapy are very good. For some organs there are special cancer nosode preparations, for example for liver tumors there is Carcinoma Hepatitis-Injeel.

Administer one drop of Glyoxal compositum until healed and of the particular nosode that corresponds to the tumor, if it is available and you are certain which organ is involved.

In addition, you should give one drop of Ubichinon compositum daily in 50 ml of drinking water.

The following serve for further support:

Tumors of the	Medicine
Liver	Carduus compositum
Kidneys	Solidago
Ovaries	Ovarium
Testes	Testis compositum
Thyroid gland	Thyreoidea compositum

Administer one drop of each daily for the first week, every three days for the second to fourth weeks, and then once a week.

Leukemic changes should be treated with Galium compositum and Lymphomyosot according to the same dosage regimen.

● Bach Flowers

Bach Flowers, Agrimony, Wild Oat, Hornbeam, and Clematis, can strengthen the will to get well and help to overcome the tumor events. Add one drop of each flower essence to 10 ml of water and administer ten drops to the bird daily in the drinking water.

When Should You Go to the Veterinarian?

You should have the bird seen by a veterinarian in order to determine if it has a tumor and what type it is to be able to target the therapy.

What Will the Veterinarian Do?

In the case of large external tumors, it may be necessary to remove these surgically in order to avoid picking and the subsequent effects. Internal tumors can usually not be operated on because of the risk of massive hemorrhage.

Prevention and Aftercare

Provide optimal living conditions (see page 12) and a diet that is appropriate for the species (see pages 16 and 20).

After cure or surgical treatment of tumor disease the bird should regularly receive the homeopathic medicines named above (once every fourteen days, later once a month).

Species Susceptibility

Basically, all birds are subject to benign and malignant tumors.

Budgerigars are especially prone to tumor formation.

Emphysema

Clinical Picture

The bird exhibits swellings or fat blisters on the upper back or distributed over the entire body. On palpation the animal feels puffy.

Sometimes there is even an audible rustling.

The general state of health can be impaired, and the bird suffers from dypsnea.

Causes

(A) An air cell has probably been torn by accident, and air has entered the surrounding tissue and is under the skin.

(B) In rare cases, Clostridium (bacteria that live without oxygen and form gases) are responsible for the air under the skin. But then the general state of health is considerably impaired.

Self-Help

(A) Disinfect the skin and, using a sterile scalpel, carefully make a tiny incision in the skin to let the air escape. Then instill Traumeel in the wound. The torn air cell will probably heal by itself after this treatment.

● **Natural Remedies**

In addition, give the bird one to two drops of Traumeel for four days.

When Should You go to the Veterinarian?

When you don't feel capable of "operating," you should not hesitate to visit a veterinarian for treatment. An operation is not everybody's thing, and it is also not entirely without risk.

If there is any suspicion of infection with Clostridium, you should go to a veterinarian.

Species Susceptibility

Emphysema occurs more often in canaries than in other species.

5

Diseases of the Extremities and the Nervous System

The wings, legs, and feet of a bird are subject to many hazards during free flight. But that should not keep you from letting your bird fly free, for free flight is a must for the health of the caged bird, and the lack of exercise is a cause for a long list of diseases.

Injuries to the Wing

These include sprains (distorsion), dislocation (luxation), and broken bones (fractures) of the wings.

Clinical Picture

The bird suddenly can't fly. One wing hangs down or is slightly spread. In other cases, the wingtips cross slightly. The affected wing can no longer be moved correctly.

During palpation, a noise (crepitation) is perceptible between the broken sections.

The bird sits quietly and slightly puffed up on its perch, its breathing is somewhat heavier.

A hanging wing indicates a break of the distal bones (radius and ulna), while a spread wing or crossed wingtips is an indication of a break in the shoulder region.

Sprains are indicated by the appearance of slight lameness and dislocations by an awkward positioning of the wing.

Also, there are often severe bruises on the underside of the wing.

Important: There are fractures of the wing bones that are not indicated by a displacement.

Causes

A break in a wing or shoulder bone is usually accident-related, as are sprains and dislocations. The bird may have been startled during free flight and flown against a windowpane or a hard corner.

A bird can even injure itself if it gets caught on a projecting corner or between cage bars.

A vigorous argument with cagemates can also be the cause.

During molting, the risk of a fracture is especially great because of the breakdown of calcium.

Self-Help

The greatest caution during an examination of the bird is urged so that a simple break or a mere crack in a bone does not become a complicated break because of the bird's resisting movements.

With open fractures and bleeding, the first measure must be to stop the bleeding with a five percent hydrogen peroxide solution.

Then gently set the injured wing in the following manner. Spread Traumeel ointment thickly on the upper and under side of the wing at the break or the sprained or dislocated joint. Then move the wing into the right position—the broken ends must fit together precisely—and fasten the injured wing and then the healthy one to the body with a gauze bandage, but not too tightly (see page 108). This bandage has the advantage of being easily removed. You can remove the bandage from the feathers with a pair of scissors.

Simple wing breaks normally knit very well within two to three weeks. With a sprain, as a rule, a week's rest is enough.

To keep parrots from immediately tearing off the bandage, it will probably be necessary to put a collar on them (see page 109).

Because a bird has difficulty keeping its balance with its wings bound, it is better to remove the perches from the cage for the first few days or to put them just above the floor so as to avoid falls. This isn't necessary with parrots, as they can hold on with their beaks.

● **Natural Remedies**

For shock, immediately administer one to two drops of Aconitum 200X if the bird is upset and skin injuries are present or one to two drops of Arnica 200X if the bird is calm and without skin injuries. Then every thirty minutes give it two drops of Traumeel. Then administer two to three drops of Traumeel daily for two weeks.

● **Bach Flowers**

In all cases of injuries or potential pain, immediately administer one to two drops of Rescue Remedy essence depending on the size of the bird, in the daily drinking water for one week.

When Should You Go to the Veterinarian?

If you suspect there is a fracture or a dislocation, you should always go to a veterinarian. After a successful treatment for shock, put the bird in a softly padded, roomy, dark container.

What Will the Veterinarian Do?

The veterinarian can better judge by means of x-rays if a fracture is present and where it is. He can also correctly set the broken bones or replace the dislocated joint.

The risk is great that a bird will no longer be able to fly properly after a wing fracture or a luxation.

A visit to a veterinarian is unavoidable with complicated or open fractures, as well as fractures near a joint, and with dislocations, because complications can occur. Often a surgical procedure is necessary.

To promote healing, the veterinarian can also order magnetic-field therapy (see page 122) for your bird.

Prevention and Aftercare

After a wing injury, the bird will have to practice flying again, very slowly at first. Give it a chance to do so without a great risk of injury.

Injuries to the Leg

Leg injuries include fractures, sprains (distortions), and dislocations (luxations).

6

Clinical Picture

The bird no longer puts weight on the injured leg. The leg can be hanging down limp and dangling or be drawn up. Sometimes the leg also swells.

In the case of complete fractures, the broken bones and their movement against each other are clearly palpable.

In an open fracture, the bones stick out of the wound.

A swelling at only one joint without a palpable fracture suggests a sprain.

If the limb has assumed an abnormal position, a dislocation must be suspected.

Causes

Such injuries usually occur during free flight. A bird can get hurt by flying into doors or drawers that are closed too quickly, by sitting on the top of a door when it is closed, or by being inadvertently stepped on by people.

When a bird is caught by its feet in the curtains, on the cage bars, or playthings, a sprain or dislocation can easily occur.

Birds with legs rings are particularly endangered in this way. If a leg ring catches in the wire of the cage, the bird could pull its foot away in a panic and break a leg bone or dislocate the leg.

Self-Help

If the leg bone is broken, it must be splinted with suitable material. Depending on the size of the bird, cut-off straws, syringes, or other quills are suitable for this purpose (for procedure, see page 108).

Toe fractures should be thickly covered with Traumeel ointment for several days. Small birds will often heal without any other measures being done.

● **Natural Remedies**

To prevent shock, immediately administer Aconitum or Arnica 200X as described on page 83, then every thirty minutes apply two drops of Traumeel. Afterwards give two to three drops of Traumeel and Zeel daily by beak for two weeks.

● **Bach Flowers**

Depending on the size of the bird, give one to two Rescue Remedy drops in the drinking water for the first few days.

When Should You Go to the Veterinarian?

After a successful treatment for shock, you should take the bird to a veterinarian in a softly padded, dark container for treatment. This is especially important if the fracture is open or complicated. It also depends on the species of bird. For parrots, surgery is often required.

Also, fractures in the muscular region of the thigh and the lower leg are hard to set and must be splinted by special techniques. The veterinarian may also recommend magnetic-field therapy (see page 122) for support.

Prevention and Aftercare

Make sure that the bird can't get caught by his leg ring. It should be neither too loose nor too tight.

Joint Inflammations

Clinical Picture

The bird favors the affected limb by not flying anymore, keeping the leg drawn up, or only gingerly putting weight on it.

With its feathers fluffed up and usually sitting on the floor, the bird shows clearly that it is not feeling well.

Palpation of the affected joint (leg, toes, wings) is very painful for the animal. The joint are swollen reddened, and feel warmer than normal. The bird can often no longer grasp the perch with its toes. Parrots hold onto the cage with their beaks in order to not fall off the perch. Some birds will pick at inflamed joints.

Causes

The problem is a joint inflammation that can have different causes.

(A) Traumatic joint inflammations are usually caused by blows, contusions, strains, or sprains. The surrounding area is also often injured, but *only one joint is affected*.

(B) Bacterial joint inflammations can be due to staphylococci, and streptococci, salmonella, and other pathogens.

All joints are affected. A bacterial infection should be suspected when the joints are hot and the general state of health is considerably altered.

(C) Among the joint inflammations resulting from metabolic disturbances are gout (see page 59) and rachitis (rickets, producing softening of the bones).

Rachitis (also osteomalacia) is caused by an absolute lack of calcium as well as other minerals and/or vitamins D_3 and B during the growing phase.

A diet solely of grain leads very quickly to rickets in young animals.

In addition to the swelling of the joints, softening of the beak and claws and a distinct malformation of the long bones and the spinal column will appear soon. Sometimes bones will break spontaneously.

A similar clinical picture can occur in adult birds because of a monotonous diet (osteomalacia), especially if they are laying eggs.

Self-Help

(A) If the joint of a wing is involved, the wing should be immobilized (see page 108) after the joint has first been thickly covered with Traumeel ointment. Leave the bandage on the bird for one week.

You should avoid a splint on the legs. Rub the joint with Traumeel and Zeel ointment daily for a week.

(B) In addition to the absolutely essential veterinary treatment, the joint can be treated with Traumeel and Zeel ointment.

(C) For treatment of gout, see page 59.

Make sure that the hospital area is quiet, warm, and dry. The affected joints can be gently massaged daily with Traumeel and Zeel ointment.

Important: It is especially important to recognize rickets early, because if the bird suffers with severe deformities of the entire skeletal system, the only thing left is to euthanize the bird.

Correct the diet by giving food that is varied and appropriate for your bird.

● **Natural Remedies**

(A) Give one drop each of Traumeel and Rhus tox-Injeel or Zeel daily for one week.

(B) In addition to the veterinary treatment, administer one drop each of Traumeel and Zeel daily until improvement.

(C) For treatment of gout, see page 59.

For support in rickets, you can administer two drops of Calcium phosphoricum-Injeel daily until improvement.

6

● **Bach Flowers**

Hornbeam and Oak can help the bird to manage its handicap better and to regain mobility. Give one drop of each in the daily drinking water.

When Should You Go to the Veterinarian?

If you suspect that your bird has bacterially caused joint inflammations, you absolutely must go to a veterinarian to find out what pathogen is causing it (risk of contagion and zoonosis!) and to institute the appropriate treatment.

If there are bone deformities arising from rachitis, the veterinarian has to decide if the animal can still be saved.

Prevention and Aftercare

(A) Insofar as possible, prevent accidents and fights for dominance!

(B) Strengthen the bird's resistance with proper living conditions (see page 12) and a nutritious diet (see page 16). Give it enough sunshine without UV-filtering panes of glass.

(C) You can prevent the occurrence of rachitis and osteomalacia by making sure that the feed has enough greens and—as a source of calcium—pulverized boiled egg, mussel, or snail shells. For several weeks, mineral and vitamin supplements should be added. You should pay special attention to calcium, as well as vitamins D_3 and B. A balanced mineral and vitamin mixture is available in specialty stores and through mail order (see page for addresses). The powdered additives must be administered with soft food because they do not adhere to grains very well.

The risk of getting rickets is especially great with hand-raised birds.

Important: Don't give a bird too much of the vitamin supplements, because overdosage can also produce a disease!

Bumblefoot

Clinical Picture

The bird no longer stands on one foot. A red, painful, and swollen area is evident, and sometimes there is a crusty sore in the center. Eventually, the joint above it and the leg will show the same symptoms.

Causes

A foot ulcer has developed because of unsuitable and dirty perches, constant pressure on the soft pad of the foot, too little exercise, being overweight, or an improper diet. Left untreated such sores lead to pressure sores and with added infections, to serious deep inflammation.

Excess mealworms in the diet may contribute to the development of sores.

Important: Never use sandpaper wrapping on the perches. A bird will quickly rub the sensitive pad of its foot raw on it.

Self-Help

Replace the old perches with sticks of wood of differing diameters that you pad further with woven tape or cotton strips. Replace the old bottom litter with a clean layer of soft, nonabrasive litter.

However, the best perches are ones of branches of nonpoisonous shrubs and trees.

Provide opportunities for free flight, as well as a balanced, bird-specific diet with vitamin A supplements (see page 16). Bathe the foot in warm water to which you may add a few drops of tea tree (Maleleuka) oil and carefully clean off any dirty and crusty scabs.

Then cover the pad with Iodoglycerine 1:2 or with tea tree oil. In addition, gently coat the inflamed area of the foot with Traumeel ointment. Repeat this procedure two or three times daily.

With larger birds you can wrap the foot with a gauze pad on which you have applied the ointment. Repeat this procedure until the foot is completely healed.

● **Natural Remedies**

Give Traumeel and Hepar sulfuris-Injeel, two drops of each daily directly in the beak, until the bird is completely healed.

When Should You Go to the Veterinarian?

If the sore develops pus or forms an abscess, the bird must be treated by a veterinarian.

Prevention and Aftercare

The most important thing is to prevent the occurrence through natural, clean perches, sufficient exercise, and the proper diet. Perches that give when they are landed on also are important.

Don't use sandpaper on perches!

Whenever you notice red, inflamed areas on your bird's feet, coat the area with Iodoglycerine immediately and then cover it with a Zinc-Cod-liver Oil ointment. At the same time, one drop each of Traumeel and Cutis compositum should be administered daily until the bird is healed.

Hyperkeratosis

Clinical Picture

On the legs and toes are thick, large horny scales that seem to enwrap the legs like splints and that considerably handicap the bird. The pressure of the deposits causes circulatory disorders. The feet can swell severely and become unable to bear weight.

Causes

Scale development is caused by the lack of opportunities for wear in caged birds, metabolic disorders, and a hereditary predisposition for the problem.

Hyperkeratosis must be differentiated from scaly leg (see page 68), a skin lesion caused by mites.

Self-Help

Coat the deposits with Iodoglycerine 1:5, and carefully try to remove the scales. Then the legs should be smeared daily with a Zinc-cod-liver-oil ointment until the bird is healed.

If a leg ring is present, it must be removed before the treatment.

● **Natural Remedies**

Administer one drop each of Traumeel and Cutis compositum daily directly in the beak.

6

Claw Deformities

Clinical Picture

The claws have lost their natural shape and grow twisted like corkscrews, bent, or severely curled over. The bird can easily get caught on them and tear them off.

Causes

Claw deformations occur through injuries, inflammations, mite and fungus diseases of the nailbed, the lack of claw care, and the lack of use from too little exercise.

Self-Help

Clip the claws to about 2 mm above the tip of the claw pith (see page 111). Any bleeding that occurs must be stopped immediately with ferric chloride. If a torn claw is not cared for immediately, the bird can bleed to death.

Treat the claw bed daily with Iodoglycerine 1:2.

● **Natural Remedies**
Give the bird one drop each of Traumeel and Graphites-Homaccord daily.

When Should You Go to the Veterinarian?

If you are not certain where to cut the deformed claws, it's better to consult a veterinarian.

Prevention and Aftercare

You can prevent deformations with regular claw care (see page 111).

Gangrene

Clinical Picture

The claws become black and fall off. The process spreads from the toes and up the leg. An inflamed area develops between the healthy and the black tissue. The affected limb is pecked at by the bird.

Causes

Severe burns and freezing can cause the necrosis. The cutting off of circulation by string or a ring that is too tight can also be responsible. Poisoning with a fungus infection or ergot can also lead to it.

Self-Help

Important: Self-help procedures are not recommended!

● **Natural Remedies**
You should administer two drops of Traumeel daily for one week in addition to the treatment provided by a veterinarian.

When Should You Go to the Veterinarian?

With the development of gangrene, you should get to a veterinarian as quickly as possible. He must decide if the bird's foot must be amputated.

Prevention and Aftercare

As much as possible, avoid wounds and cutting off circulation in the toes that can lead to the death of tissue.

Lameness and Paralysis of the Peripheral Nervous System

Symptoms of lameness and complete paralysis usually develop over a long period of time.

Clinical Picture

At first, the bird is a little unsteady on its legs. Soon it can no longer hold onto the perch and only crouches on the floor. If both legs are affected, it can only lie on the ground. Parrots hold onto the bars of the cage with their beaks so they will not fall down.

Externally, the extremities appear unchanged.

With pressure on the foot, you can test the grasping reflex, an involuntary muscle contraction of the toes. With lameness it is hesitating, and with paralysis it isn't present at all. Often, disturbances in balance occur simultaneously.

If the wings are affected, they can no longer be used.

Causes

Symptoms of paralysis of one limb can be the consequence of fractures, joint and muscle inflammations, or bruises. The particular nerves involved are damaged by stretching, bruising, and in severe cases tearing.

Also, tumors can press on a nerve and, in time, block the entire pathway.

In some cases, a deficiency of the supply of vitamins B and E can cause the symptoms of paralysis.

Self-Help

If the bird can no longer stand, you should pad the bottom of the cage with a thick, soft cellulose padding. If it no longer wants or is able to take food on its own, you must give it food and water by hand. Above all, the B-complex vitamins should be added to the water.

● Natural Remedies

Give one drop each of Traumeel, Nux vomica-Homaccord, and Gelsemium 30X three to four times daily. After two days you should switch to Argentum nitricum 30X and Ignatia 200X (or Ignatia-Injeel). If an injury is present, you can also use Rhus tox-Injeel. Give one drop of each per day by mouth.

● Bach Flowers

Dilute one drop of Rescue Remedy Essence with 5 ml of water and administer several drops a number of times daily for support of the bird.

Alternatively, you can mix two drops of the Rescue Remedy essence into the drinking water daily.

Important: The treatment of paralyses requires a considerable amount of patience. Sometimes there is an improvement or healing only after many weeks.

When Should You Go to the Veterinarian?

To clarify the reasons for the paralysis and be able to treat it appropriately, you should consult a veterinarian.

Prevention and Aftercare

With a varied diet that is correct for your bird (see page 16), you can prevent deficiencies that can lead to paralyses.

6

Paralysis and Convulsions in the Central Nervous System

Clinical Picture

Diseases of the central nervous system can manifest themselves in very different clinical pictures:

—The bird lies completely unconscious on the ground.

—The bird suffers from violent convulsive attacks from time to time, with involvement of the entire body.

—The bird compulsively turns its head upward.

Causes

The diseases of the central nervous system affect the brain and spinal cord. One of the causes is a brain concussion from a collision with a window or the cage bars. The bird may even have received a skull fracture or contusion of the brain or spinal cord.

Other possible triggers of the diseases are poisoning (metallic toxins are particularly dangerous for birds), infections with bacteria, viruses, or fungi; deficiencies of the B complex vitamins and vitamin E; tumors; and circulatory disturbances.

Self-Help

If you know that an accident has occurred, don't move the bird unnecessarily. Lay it on a cloth in quiet, warm, slightly darkened surroundings.

Follow the same procedure for convulsions.

● Natural Remedies

For all disorders of the central nervous system you should use Cerebrum compositum and Traumeel. Try to instill one drop of each of them every half hour into the injured bird.

After a collapse, first give two drops of Carbo vegetabilis 200X every half hour by mouth. When the bird opens its eyes again, administer one to two drops of Sulfur 200X every three hours.

● Bach Flowers

Rescue Remedy drops are indicated for all accidents. They contribute to the bird's ability to overcome the shock well. Apply one drop to the middle of the head.

When Should You Go to the Veterinarian?

If you suspect the bird has an infectious disease, you should consult a veterinarian. The same goes for all disorders whose causes you cannot explain.

Prevention and Aftercare

Try to avoid accidents like flying against a window by putting curtains in front of the window and making sure that the bird cannot be frightened during free flight.

Make sure that the bird can't ingest any poisonous materials. (See Poisoning, page 99.)

Be sure you feed the bird a nutritious, vitamin-rich diet containing enough B-vitamins (see page 16).

Species Susceptibility

All bird species can suffer from diseases of the peripheral and central nervous systems.

Behavioral Disorders

Behavioral disorders and neuroses are a common problem in pet birds. But many of these difficulties could be avoided if the animals were kept in the most appropriate sized cage for their species and not kept alone (see page 12).

The most striking and the best studied are the mental problems of parrots. Because of their intelligence, playfulness, and capability for imitation, they are particularly popular as pets. But while they, being very social birds, live in large groups in nature, they often live alone in captivity. Without a partner to communicate with and to play with, a great many problems arise. If the birds do not succeed in adapting to their environment and the lifestyle in captivity, out of loneliness and boredom they develop compulsive behavioral patterns or they become generally ill and finally die.

It is often said that parrots kept alone become tame faster and learn to speak better or that the male canary supposedly only sings when he is kept alone. This is false, for the most part. Parrots kept in a community can also become tame and speak; however, it does usually require somewhat more patience. It can possibly be of advantage to keep a very young bird alone temporarily until he is tame. Canaries also sing in the company of other male canaries and female canaries—probably only somewhat more seldom. But they feel considerably better!

Hand-raised parrots are strongly imprinted to humans. However, this leads to correspondingly undesirable activities in the bird later, at the development of sexual maturity. The human will hardly be in a position to replace the natural life-partner of the bird around the clock.

Feather Plucking

Feather plucking to the point of almost complete baldness seems to many parrot owners a problem without an apparent solution. There is really not a disease involved here but a deep-seated behavioral disorder that has its roots in captivity and unfavorable living conditions.

This neurosis is the most striking and the best known. It can lead to self-mutilation.

Clinical Picture

Normal plumage grooming gradually escalates into excessive and aggressive biting and pulling out of feathers. At first the bird only pulls out a few feathers playfully. But then it becomes a regular addiction, to which the entire plumage is sacrificed. Usually the bird begins to pull the feathers out of its breast; then it doesn't take long before it is sitting there on the perch plucked bald. Only the head remains covered with feathers, because the bird can't reach those. The naked bird with a feathered head is a typical indication of feather plucking. In contrast, birds who lose their feathers through diseases, such as feather-loss syndrome (see page 75), also lose the feathers on their head.

Sometimes the nail or even the toes and other soft parts are diligently gnawed by the bird.

Commonly, earlier—perhaps unnoticed—stages of the neurosis have preceded the feather plucking, such as increased busyness with toys, constant compulsive leaping from perch to perch, constant back-and-forth motions of the head, nervousness, or exaggerated jumpiness.

Causes

Boredom and loneliness, perhaps grief for a lost partner (bird or human), are usually the grounds for the development of this neurosis. Too small a cage, unsuitable toys, always the same view, lack of free flight, wrong perches, being left alone, and not enough attention from the owner all contribute to the problem.

Many birds are very sensitive and react quickly with a psychological disorder when, for instance, something changes in their environment or when there has been an addition to the family.

Important: Feather loss and feather plucking can also have other causes. Therefore, infectious disease, such as ornithosis/psitticosis or PBFD, ectoparasites like chicken mites, endoparasites like *Giardia*, severe deficiency conditions, metabolic disturbances, or tumors should be ruled out first.

Self-Help

If you are certain that feather plucking has psychological grounds, you must first consider the living conditions of your bird and change them (see page 12). Give your bird a roomy cage with perches of natural wood, things to climb on, and places to hide. Put the cage where things are going on and the bird is not alone. There should not be more than eight to twelve hours worth of daylight daily. If this is the case, the cage should be covered with a thick cover.

Give your bird the opportunities for daily free flight and bathing.

It is of utmost importance that you try to provide the bird with a partner that it will accept. In this, parrots of different species can also develop sympathetic relationships with one another, for example, amazons and budgerigars.

For your bird's diet, place a great emphasis on providing a balance of protein, minerals, and vitamins.

● **Bach Flowers**

Mix one drop each of the Bach Flower essences, Rock Water, Hornbeam, Mustard, Chestnut Bud, Willow, and Water Violet, with 10 ml of water. Administer two to four drops, according to the size of the bird, four times a day if possible.

But alternatively, you can add one drop of each of them to the daily drinking water.

As a supportive measure, mix several drops of the essences in ½ l of water and spray the bird with it daily.

The Bach Flowers can help the bird overcome its compulsive activity and depressed condition and to find its way back to its carefree state.

If the bird has just recently come to live with you, you should give it Walnut so it can more easily accept its new environment.

When Should You Go to the Veterinarian?

To be sure that there is no contagious infection, parasite, or other physical ailment behind the feather plucking, you should consult a veterinarian.

Prevention and Aftercare

Avoid the causes like incorrect maintenance and feeding! Make sure that the parrot is not separated from its partner or primary care person.

More patience is necessary in order to finally break the parrot of the habit that has turned obsessional. Give the bird more attention, but not when it has just pulled out feathers. This will only strengthen the habit. When you catch the bird pulling feathers, you can put a cover over the cage for a few minutes.

Species Susceptibility

Feather plucking and self-mutilation are primarily seen with parrots and cockatoos.

Dominant Behavior

Birds are fiercely territorial and develop a strict pecking order when they live in group aviaries.

But dominant behavior can become a problem when one bird in the group acts very aggressively.

Clinical Picture

(A) The bird constantly torments another, subordinate bird.
(B) The bird acts dominant and aggressive with its keeper. It may even happen that it toler-

ates being held by the keeper and responds aggressively to other members of the family. Bites, especially by the larger parrots, can have bad consequences.

Causes

(A) The birds don't get along with each other and are unsympathetic.
(B) Dominant behavior toward the keeper could possibly occur if the bird is constantly sitting above the height of the keeper's head.

Self-Help

(A) Separate the birds.
(B) Behavioral scientists recommend putting the cage and perches for the bird below the chest level of the animal keeper. However, the perches should not be below waist level, because the bird can develop an anxiety neurosis. Sometimes you can effectively defend against attacks by a bird with a water pistol. It is also recommended that you don't give the bird its entire ration of food at once all the time. Instead, give some of it first out of your hand, if the bird will let itself be touched. Biting is a natural behavior pattern of parrots. From the very beginning, therefore, a young bird must be consistently trained that it must not bite.

● Bach Flowers
For support, you should add one drop of Beech to the daily drinking water. This Bach Flower especially soothes animals that are characterized by intolerance and dominance.

Also, Vervain, Vine, and Holly—one drop of each in the drinking water—help to change the bird's dominant and aggressive behavior.

7

Prevention and Aftercare

Provide species-appropriate living conditions and above all, do not keep only one bird (see page 12)! Observe your bird daily to see if it is getting along with the other birds in the group.

Species Susceptibility

Young amazons have the reputation for easily developing into "tyrants."

Screaming

The prolonged, neurotic screaming of some parrots is certainly the behavioral disorder that most stresses the nerves of the owner.

Clinical Picture

The bird screams long and continuously and will not be quieted.

Causes

Screaming is really a very normal means of expression and behavior in parrots. They greet every day with a cry and express their joy at a reunion with loud screams.

However, it can become intolerable when the bird screams constantly as an expression of loneliness, grief, boredom, frustration, or anxiety.

Some birds also scream to get the attention of their owner.

Self-Help

If possible, provide a partner for your bird and provide variety and conversation.

If the screaming in a newly acquired bird is an expression of warning and anxiety as soon as you come near it, you must not pay any attention to it. Otherwise the bird will get the idea that screaming works. In spite of its screams, quietly offer it treats by hand.

In birds who make a scene to be noticed, it is important that you don't take any notice of the bird as long as it is screaming. For that will only strengthen the undesirable behavior in the future. On the other hand, it would also be wrong to scold the bird so that the screamer has gotten what he wanted—attention.

Important: You cannot and must not inhibit joyful screaming in greeting! Go quickly to your bird and greet it just as joyfully.

● Bach Flowers

For screams of fear give Mimulus, Aspen, and Sweet Chestnut. To ease the bird's acclimation to its new surroundings and overcome grief, it should receive Walnut and Honeysuckle.

If the screaming appears to be an expression of a compulsive neurosis, Rock Water, Chestnut Bud, and Gentian will help. Give one drop of each in the daily drinking water.

Prevention and Aftercare

A significant amount of patience is required to stop excessive screaming. Reward your bird when it doesn't scream and punish it with ignoring it, or cover the cage when screaming is prolonged. You can also put the cage in another room until the animal stops screaming. When the bird has stopped screaming, you should give it intensive attention as a reward for agreeable behavior.

Sexual Problems

Normally, the male regurgitates food as part of courtship to feed his "idol."

Clinical Picture

(A) In the absence of a true bird partner, male birds primarily tend to regurgitate food over substitute objects. The bird "vomits" on his own plumage, on mirrors, toys, another bird, or the arm of the keeper. He can also attempt to mate.

(B) Unpartnered female birds constantly lay numerous eggs.

Causes

Birds have a powerful reproductive drive and being kept partnerless leads to behavioral problems in both sexes.

(A) The bird has chosen his toys, a same-sex bird, or the keeper as substitute partner. The regurgitation of a food slurry as courtship food represents a special declaration of love.

(B) The female bird has probably sought the keeper as partner. Disturbances of hormone balances will occur.

Also, ovarian tumors can manifest themselves this way.

Self-Help

(A) It would be best if you would provide your bird with an appropriate partner. If this is not possible, as a helping measure, you should remove all objects that the bird "feeds" from the cage for the time being.

(B) Don't take the eggs away from the hen. That will only make it keep laying compulsively. If it can go through an entire brooding cycle, often the problems subside—at least temporarily. Finally, remove the nest.

● **Natural Remedies**

For regulation of the hormone balance, give the hen one drop each of Ovarium compositum, Hormeel, and Cerebrum compositum daily by mouth for seven days.

● **Bach Flowers**

Of the Bach Flowers, Hornbeam and Impatiens may be able to help the bird to cope with the inappropriate circumstances of its life. A misimprinted bird is helped by Cerato—one drop in the drinking water daily—to transfer to the right partner.

When Should You Go to the Veterinarian?

If necessary, a veterinarian can intervene with hormones.

Prevention and Aftercare

Don't keep birds singly. Keep them in pairs, at least.

Species Susceptibility

Both disorders are often observed in budgerigars, but they also occur in other bird species.

7

Emergencies

Accidents

Accidents are usually the result of human carelessness. For example, the bird can get stepped on or caught in a closing door. But life-threatening situations can also arise if the bird flies against a windowpane. There can be massive trauma in the beak, head, and eye regions. Often there is a concussion.

The bird is unconscious and very quickly goes into shock.

Emergency Measures

Move the bird very carefully and place it on a soft surface in quiet, warm surroundings.

Stop bleeding immediately by dabbing with ferric chloride.

● **Natural Remedies**
Immediately administer one to two drops of Carbo vegetabilis 200x and, when the bird regains consciousness, one drop each of Cerebrum compositum and Traumeel every half hour.

● **Bach Flowers**
Administer one drop of Rescue Remedy to the bird's head and one to five drops, depending on the size of the bird, of the diluted solution (one drop in 5 ml of water).

When the general condition has stabilized, go to a veterinarian.

Hemorrhages

Small birds, especially, have very little blood (ten percent of the body weight) and with a wound can quickly go into life-threatening shock and bleed to death.

Emergency Measures

You must bring minor bleeding to a standstill at once by swabbing the bleeding area with ferric chloride or hydrogen peroxide. To stop larger wounds from hemorrhaging, apply a pressure bandage directly on the source of the bleeding, or apply a tourniquet above the wound to stop the flow.

When the bleeding has stopped, coat the wound area with Traumeel ointment.

● **Natural Remedies**
Administer two drops Traumeel to the bird every thirty minutes.

● **Bach Flowers**
Rescue Remedy drops help to overcome the shock of the injury. Dilute the essence (one drop in 5 ml of water) and give two to four drops, according to size, every hour.

Burns and Scalds

Birds that fly free in the house are unfortunately afflicted by these injuries relatively frequently.

Clinical Picture

Depending on the degree of the burn, at the burn site you will see reddening of the skin, formation of blisters, or yellowish-gray scabbing all the way up to necrotized tissue. Often the entire legs are affected. The legs swell severely and are very pain-sensitive. The general state of health is considerably disturbed.

Extensive burns can easily lead to death. Burned toes are likely to necrotize and fall off.

Causes

Birds that fly free indoors, especially the confident and curious parrots, are endangered by hot burners, lamps, halogen lamps, candles, boiling liquids, hot oil, and hot steam.

Emergency Measures

Immediately hold the burned area under running cold water. Clinging oil should be carefully washed off. Keep cooling the burns constantly, and supply the patient with plenty of fluids.

Carefully coat the burned skin areas with Glycerine or Traumeel ointment (preferably with a cotton swab).

The affected areas should then be treated twice a day with Traumeel ointment.

● Bach Flowers

Immediately after the accident give the bird Rescue Remedy Drops in diluted form (two drops in 5 ml of water) both externally on the burned areas and internally, two to four drops (depending on the size of the bird) every fifteen minutes at first.

They help to overcome the shock and give the cells a stimulus to resume their daily activity.

● Natural Remedies

Make a mixture (of equal parts) of Traumeel, Causticum compositum, and Echinacea compositum, and give the bird two to four drops (depending on bird's size) every half hour at first, later at longer intervals.

If the patient drinks, you can also give it five drops of the mixture in about 10 ml of water.

After the third day, give the bird Traumeel, Cutis compositum, Carduus compositum, and Coenzyme compositum (same dosage as above) twice daily.

When Should You Go to the Veterinarian?

With severe burns you should always take the bird to a veterinarian immediately after first aid treatment.

Prevention and Aftercare

Only let your bird fly free when there are no heat sources in use, such as pots, lamps, or candles.

Freezing

Birds that live in outdoor aviaries without frost-free shelters are affected during severe cold weather.

Clinical Picture

Frozen places on the body, especially the feet, are strikingly pale and then turn blue-red. They are either swollen and hot or cold and very painful. As with a burn, blisters and sores can

8

develop. The tissue can become necrotic. Because of the severe itching, the bird scratches its toes with its beak, which can cause severe bleeding.

Causes

Freezing, primarily of the legs and toes, usually occurs if the birds are startled out of their warm shelter during severe cold, fly against the icy cage wire and hold on to it, or sit for a long time against the ice-cold caging.

Freezing can also occur when a bird kept in an outdoor aviary takes its daily bath during freezing weather in its warm drinking water. When it climbs on the cold cage wires the wet feet freeze.

The feathered skin is less at risk.

Emergency Measures

Bring the bird inside into a frost-free but cool room. Areas that are freshly frozen are best washed first with cold water.

Gently treat the affected area repeatedly with Traumeel ointment.

● Natural Remedies
Mix Traumeel, Echinacea compositum, Cutis compositum, Carduus compositum, and Coenzyme compositum in equal parts, and give the bird two to four drops (depending on size) hourly; from the second day only twice daily.

● Bach Flowers
With severe freezing, immediately treat externally and internally with diluted Rescue Drops as described under Burns on page 97.

When Should You Go to the Veterinarian?

This type of injury should be examined by a veterinarian.

Precautions and Aftercare

Prevent your birds from flying against the cage wires, especially on very cold winter nights. Either don't let the birds out of the frost-protected area or you must protect the inside of the caging with cloths or planks or cardboard. A fundamental requirement in an outdoor aviary is a protected, warm, and dry area where the birds can shelter. Keep a bird that has been frozen in isolation so the other cage- or aviary-mates won't peck at the injured places.

Important: In the wintertime, only give the birds drinking water in dishes in which they cannot bathe.

Circulatory Failure and Collapse

The bird suddenly breathes shallowly and fast, sits on the floor, or lies on its side.

Emergency Measures

Transport the bird in a dark, softly padded, sufficiently large and well-ventilated container to the veterinarian immediately after the general condition is stabilized.

● **Natural Remedies**

Before transporting the bird, as a first aid measure immediately give it one to two drops of Carbo vegetabilis 200x or Carbo vegetabilis-Injeel.

● **Bach Flowers**

In addition, use Rescue Remedy Drops internally and externally for stabilization. Depending on the size of the bird, give two to four drops of the dilution (two drops of essence to 5 ml of water).

Heat Stroke

The bird sits or lies on the ground and breathes fast and shallowly.

Emergency Measures

Immediately place the bird in a darkened, cool room and spray it with finely vaporized cool water in which you have mixed some drops of Rescue Remedy.

● **Natural Remedies**

Immediately administer one to two drops of Aconitum-Injeel and Carbo vegetabilis 200x; repeat this procedure after fifteen minutes.

When the condition has stabilized, you should have the bird examined by a veterinarian.

Poisoning

Poisonings in birds very often lead to rapid death or to severe liver and kidney damage.

Sometimes the symptoms will be vomiting and/or diarrhea or local caustic burns and skin irritations.

A bird can be poisoned by:
—rat and mouse poison
—solder or old paint on cages
—pressure-treated wood
—cleaning materials, disinfectants, insecticides, or mothballs
—petroleum, paint, and paint removers
—lead curtain weights
—medications, contaminated food and water, salt (a mere 0.14 oz [4 g] for a bird weighing 2 lb [1 kg] is lethal!)
—too many mealworms, hemp, or greens that have been sprayed with pesticides
—poisonous plants, such as dieffenbachia, philodendron, azalea, or cyclamen
—tobacco, alcohol, or steam from Teflon pans.
Usually you can only suspect poisoning.

Emergency Measures

As fast as possible after first aid treatment, get the bird to a veterinarian in a large, darkened container.

● **Natural Remedies**

Immediately give the bird one drop each of Nux vomica-Homaccord, Carduus compositum, and Coenzyme compositum and possibly Arsenicum album-Injeel as well.

You should carry out this therapy for two weeks.

● **Bach Flowers**

In support of the treatment also give the bird two to four drops of the diluted Rescue Remedy Essence (two drops in 5 ml of water).

8

Important: Only collect fresh green in places where you can be certain that they have not been sprayed and that they have not been exposed to too many car exhaust gases.

Egg-Binding

Clinical Picture

A female bird tries in vain with severe straining of the abdominal wall to expel an egg stuck in the oviduct. She is restless, sits on her perch with legs spread or even on the ground in a corner, beats her tail, eventually utters a soft, mournful peeping, and her wings hang down.

The stool is often mixed with blood or there can even be no more stool expelled.

If the egg-binding lasts over a long period, there can be severe disturbances of the general state of health, with dypsnea. The bird is exhausted and very vulnerable to shock.

Causes

Egg-binding can have several causes.

In young birds that are laying an egg for the first time, an immature oviduct with too narrow a birth canal can be responsible.

Cold and vitamin deficiency favor egg-binding.

Malformed or soft-shelled eggs can become stuck in the oviduct.

Emergency Measures

Warmth (for example, an infrared light) and high humidity often help. With large birds you can try to carefully massage the egg along. If the egg appears in the cloacal region, an attempt can be made to remove the egg manually with the help of olive oil or enemas and warmth. If it breaks in the process, you must carefully remove the pieces with tweezers.

Then treat the interior of the cloaca and the anal area for three to four days with Traumeel ointment.

● **Natural Remedies**
Give young birds whose sex organs may not be completely developed one drop each of Pulsatilla 4X and Mucosa compositum daily, preferably several days before egg laying.

If egg-binding is suspected, administer one drop each of Pulsatilla 4X, Gelsemium-Homaccord, and Chamomilla-Injeel forte every fifteen to thirty minutes. This medicine resolves spasms and loosens and promotes contractions.

In advanced stages or when you intervene manually, you must also carry out supporting circulatory therapy with Cor compositum, Carduus compositum, and Coenzyme compositum and prevent shock with Carbo vegetabilis-Injeel, Aconitum-Injeel, and/or Arnica 30X.

Give one drop of each of the substances named, and repeat the therapy every thirty minutes as necessary.

● **Bach Flowers**
Because this is a matter of true emergency, you should use the Rescue Remedy Drops. They help the bird to surmount the crisis. Dilute one drop of Rescue Remedy with one ml of water, and give the hen two drops of it several times. In addition, you can drip a drop on the skin of her head.

Also helpful in egg-binding is one drop Wild Chestnut in 10 ml of water.

Important: If the patient is hand-shy, avoid the additional excitement and try to carry out the therapy through the drinking water (if it drinks). The danger that the bird will suffer shock and die is great.

When Should You Go to the Veterinarian?

If the egg doesn't come for hours, can't be moved along with careful massage, and the bird acts exhausted, you absolutely must get the bird to a veterinarian.

Prevention and Aftercare

Don't let birds that are too young mate.

Make sure there is adequate provision of vitamins and minerals and enough warmth.

Avoid stress from overcrowding.

Drowning

The confident and curious budgerigars and other parrots unfortunately often fall into filled bathtubs, pots, watering cans, or open toilets.

They cannot get out by themselves and are in danger of drowning.

Emergency Measures

Hold the bird upside down and try to remove any water that is in the airway by swinging downward movements of the hand. Slight pressure on the body may perhaps also bring water out. Then take the bird, warmly wrapped, to a veterinarian as fast as possible.

● **Bach Flowers**

Immediately give one drop of Rescue Remedy on the head or on the skin at the underside of the wings to help with shock.

Flypaper Trap

The bird that flies around freely in the house gets caught on flypaper. If you have birds that are allowed to fly free in the house *do not* use the kind of fly and insect traps that consist of glue-covered paper strips. If, however, a small birds contacts a type of glue strip, proceed as follows: Carefully cut the strip, and cut away as much of the glue strip as possible. If necessary clip away feathers with glue on them. Remove the remaining glue with a dab of "glue off" or with a small amount of cleaning fluid. Be careful not to get the chemical agents near the nares and on the skin.

Emergency Measures

Wash the feathers thoroughly with lukewarm water and a gentle, organic detergent.

Rinse several times with clear water. Make sure that all chemicals, glue, and detergent are thoroughly removed.

Put the bird in a warm, quiet room to dry (possibly set up an infrared lamp).

● **Bach Flowers**

Dilute one drop of Rescue Remedy with 1 ml of water and, to prevent shock, immediately give the bird two drops in the beak and externally under the wings.

8

Techniques for the Bird Owner

The healthy maintenance of a bird is the wish of any responsible animal keeper. On the following pages you will learn how you can recognize diseases early enough, how to examine the bird properly, and how to feed it in case of illness. There also are some tips and trips on preventive care measures, the right treatment for injuries, and the administration of medications.

Technique

The Examination

If your bird suddenly is sitting there more quietly than usual, taking no interest in anything, refusing food or water, or the consistency of its stool has changed (color, form, smell), you should examine it carefully. This begins with careful observation of the bird in its current surroundings without upsetting it by touching it.

Catching the Bird

If the patient won't voluntarily come to your hand for a thorough examination, you must carefully and quickly catch it. It is easier if you remove the objects from the cage first except for one or two perches and then darken the room. Only leave a red or a blue light burning, for you will able to see well enough, but the bird won't. Then move your hand closer, without making any noise

and without frightening it, and grasp it from behind.

If the room or the cage cannot be darkened, try to catch the bird with a cloth in one corner. To do so, throw the cloth over the bird. When you have the bird in your hand, you must not press too hard on its chest, because in sensitive birds this can cause respiratory arrest and death.

Preliminaries to Examination

For the examination, take the bird in your left hand with the bird on its back, and hold the head between your thumb and forefinger.

Be careful of the powerful beak and ferocious claws of the large parrots like the aras or cockatoos! Remember that this bird, as a professional nutcracker, can bite right through your fingers. Therefore, it is safer to quickly wrap a parrot in a thick hand towel and to grasp the bird and towel firmly from behind with your index finger and thumb. Don't let it go again!

A really reliable assistant is an advantage here.

If you want to be sure to keep the parrot from biting, you can make use of a drastic method for a short time. Let the bird bite a thick stick and then quickly and carefully but firmly wrap a string around upper and lower beak (see drawing), and tie its beak closed.

This is the way to hold the bird for examination. Be careful not to press too hard on the ribcage!

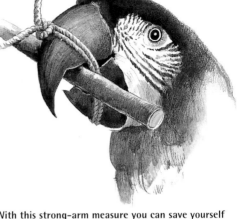

With this strong-arm measure you can save yourself from making unpleasant acquaintance with the powerful parrot beak during an examination.

Carefully immobilize parrots with help of a hand towel.

This method is also useful if you must force-feed the parrot.

The Examination

Now an assessment of the plumage is possible. Blow gently against the feathers. This lets you easily examine the skin underneath them. The examination continues, beginning with the head. Check the nostrils and beak, then the eyes and the conjunctiva. After opening the beak, inspect the tongue, mucous membranes, and throat.

Then carefully palpate the bird's neck and chest with your thumb and index finger and then using light pressure with your index finger examine the entire surface of the abdominal region. Then the anus, cloaca, and back area should be examined.

The extremities are also examined by palpation. Slide the wings and legs between your thumb and index finger. Finally, you should check the toes.

The entire examination must be handled extremely carefully so a weakened bird doesn't suffer sudden death from shock.

Important: Body temperature and pulse cannot be measured in birds. The body temperature of a healthy bird ranges between 104° and 111°F (40° and 44°C), depending on the species; the heart rate ranges between 110 and 600 beats per minute, depending on size and degree of excitement!

Technique

Recognizing Illnesses

Every living organism is constantly exposed to internal and external stimuli to which it reacts in order to reach and maintain a condition of equilibrium. This condition is termed healthiness, but it possesses no firm boundaries. Transitions are gradual. If the equilibrium is disturbed, the organism's powers of resistance are correspondingly reduced. The first signs of illness appear because germs can reproduce unhindered.

External changes, for example in plumage, skin, beak, and legs, can be easily recognized. Internal sufferings, on the other hand, are often only surmised without further diagnostic aids, because birds cannot be examined as thoroughly as dogs or cats.

This bird is sick. This can be seen clearly by its fluffed-up feathers.

Fluffed-Up Feathers

If a bird is fluffed up, possibly even sticking its head under its feathers, it is clearly indicating that it is sick and has an increased need for warmth. Therefore, as a first aid measure, you should be sure the bird gets sufficient warmth, for example, with an infrared lamp (see page 109).

If you keep several birds and the others show similar symptoms, you must consider an epizootic disease or poisoning (see page 99).

Gummy Nose and Eyes

Damp, dirty, or gummy nostrils suggest a disease of the upper airway, for example, a cold (see page 44). At the same time the bird shakes its head and picks its nose with its toenails.

If, in addition, the general state of health is impaired, the feathers are fluffed up, and the eyes may also be gummy, a disease of the lower airway must be considered (see page 45).

Dirty Cloaca

If the cloaca is dirty or reddened, an inflammation of the cloaca itself or of the intestine may be present.

Additional indications are the condition of the stool. If the excretions appear normal (see below), an inflammation is probably limited to the cloaca. If the fecal portion (the "true" feces) of the stool has changed color, is thinner than usual, is smeary, and is mixed with the urine portion, the bird has diarrhea (see page 52). Polyuria (see Kidney Inflammation, page 107) must be distinguished from this!

The excreta of a healthy bird consist of two well-differentiated constituents, the dark, brown-green feces and the white, creamy uric acid. In most grain eaters, the feces are pasty in shape, whereas in soft-food eaters it is rather soupy and of a wet consistency.

Kidney Inflammation

With a kidney inflammation the true stool from the intestine is normal in shape (see above), but the urine portion is watery and morbidly increased (polyuria). Urate (whitish uric acid) and urine are mixed with one another. On a piece of paper or cellulose you can clearly see how the urine portion flows. For kidney inflammation, see page 57.

Weight Loss or Obesity

During the examination of the breast you can assess the dietary status of the bird and any possible hidden metabolic disturbances. Normally, the breast of a healthy, well-nourished bird is slightly rounded and smooth.

If the breastbone is very prominent, the bird is undernourished and has already been sick for a long time. Besides metabolic disturbances, this can also be an indication of endoparasites.

If the breast is entirely flat on one side but is rounded on the other, this can be the result of a functional disorder of the particular wing (e.g., fracture, sprain, or joint inflammation).

If the breast clearly bulges outward, perhaps even with palpable deposits, the bird is too fat. This is an indication of overfeeding, lack of exercise, and possibly hypothyroidism.

Important: In examining for the dietary status, you must never press too firmly on the ridge of the breastbone, because you can interfere with your bird's breathing.

A dragging wing is a sign of a broken wing.

Motor Disturbances

Lameness, an uncertain stance, a hanging wing, and an inability to fly indicate a disorder of the locomotor system (e.g., joint gout, inflammation of the joint, see pages 59, 84; sprain, dislocation, fracture, see pages 82 and 83).

Careful examination in your hand can provide additional findings.

Sudden paralyses also suggest poisoning (see pages 90, 99) or a virus infection.

Slowly developing paralyses can be tumor-related (see page 79) or the result of a deficiency disease.

Technique

Practical Assistance

With small birds, in an emergency, you can splint a simple or closed fracture of a leg bone or a wing yourself—provided you have enough experience. The same goes for sprains (see pages 82 and 83).

Important: In principle, fractures should be treated by a veterinarian!

Splinting a Leg

If a leg bone is broken, it must be splinted with suitable material. Depending on the size of the bird, you can use shortened drinking straws, syringes or other sleeves, but toothpicks with the sharp points broken off or quills of feathers may also work.

Spread the areas of fracture thickly with Traumeel; then bring the two ends of the bones together in the correct position. The prepared splints are then positioned from the toes to the next joint, padded at the ends with a little cotton, and immobilized with tape for two to three weeks.

Bandaging a Broken Wing

You must immobilize a broken wing after you have carefully brought the broken ends of the bones together in the correct position.

Fix the injured and the healthy wing to the body by winding a gauze bandage crosswise between the bird's legs and knotting them on the back. In so doing you must be careful to leave the legs and the cloaca clear and that the ban-

With a stiff support, e.g., a straw and tape, a break in a leg bone is splinted.

The bandage for immobilization of the broken wing must not constrict the bird. Legs and cloaca must remain clear.

A so-called Elizabethan collar cut from a piece of plastic (also available in pet stores) keeps the parrot from chewing on the bandage.

dage isn't too tight and thus hindering the bird from breathing and eating properly.

The bandage has the advantage of being very easy to remove.

Depending on the species of the bird, it can be necessary to put tape over the bandage. However, be careful that it doesn't stick to the feathers, because that will cause unnecessary problems with removal.

It is wise to fix the wingtips to the tail with another small bandage for security.

With a complicated fracture or if the bones don't knit together properly, it is possible that the bird may be unable to fly again. Therefore,

when there is any doubt, it's better to go to a veterinarian!

Applying a Collar

To keep parrots from gnawing the bandage off, an expanded plastic collar must be applied. For this, a piece of firm expanded plastic is cut to the appropriate size, laid loosely around the neck, and fastened together.

A collar can be obtained from a pet store or from a veterinarian.

Important: Make sure the collar is loose and the bird is not prevented from eating or breathing.

Warming a Bird

If a bird has fluffed-up feathers, is sniffling, or has egg-binding, warmth will do it good. Set up an infrared lamp (150 to 250 watts) at a distance of 12 to 16 in (30 to 40 cm) from the cage. A part of the cage should be left unirradiated so that the bird can find a cooler place if it needs to. The temperature in the irradiated circle should not go over 95°F (35°C). When the bird gets better, slowly reduce the temperature by increasing the distance between the lamp and the cage.

In a pinch, a heating pad or even a hot-water bottle that you put under the sand can give the bird the necessary warmth.

Always provide higher humidity at the same time by hanging a damp cloth in the cage.

Important: In cases of lameness or paralysis, however, additional warmth can be harmful.

Technique

Preventive Care Measures

Birds don't present any large demands with regard to body care. Usually, they do it themselves if they have the opportunity to.

For example, a sticky beak is polished on the perch or a rough stone. Also, the claws are worn down on the perches of natural branches of different sizes or on the cage floor itself.

However, some care measures are also necessary to maintain the health of your feathered friend in captivity.

Beak Care

With parrots it is wise to paint the beak and cere once a week with Iodoglycerine or Tea Tree Oil. This keeps the beak elastic and shining and prevents beak mites and fungus infection.

Regularly inspect the beak for deformities (see page 37). You should carry out any corrective procedures about every four weeks so the bird's ingestion of food is not interfered with, it can continue to groom itself, and it will not injure itself. It is easiest with a high-speed drilling machine. But let a veterinarian show you the technique the first time. If you don't trust yourself to do the job, it's better if you go to a veterinarian each time.

With grain eaters and soft-food eaters, beak care is only necessary in rare cases.

Nose Care

Parrots that are kept in the house should have a nasal irrigation every two to four weeks because of the dry, dusty air. Depending on the size of the bird, one to five drops of saline solution should be instilled in each nostril. The bird should draw the drops into its nose. This will clean the mucous membrane, and an irritation of the mucous membrane will be prevented.

Important: All bird species that are kept indoors will benefit from a weekly fogging of the cage with a saline solution in order to moisten the air and the airway. It will not harm the plumage.

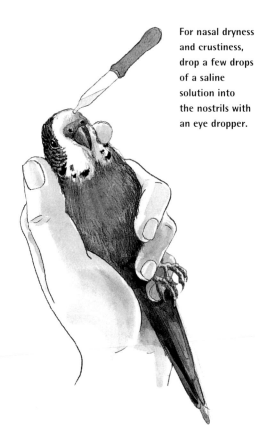

For nasal dryness and crustiness, drop a few drops of a saline solution into the nostrils with an eye dropper.

Plumage Care

To care for the plumage and skin, you should spray your bird once weekly with an organic, nontoxic mite spray. This will help prevent attacks of external parasites and fungus.

With disorders of the uropygeal gland, the feathers should be moistened at least twice a week with this spray.

Another important part of plumage care is an adequately large bird bath that is deep enough for the bird to be able to get wet all over without drowning. Birds from the humid tropical areas are especially grateful if they can bathe once a day in lukewarm water sprayed from above. The water washes away the remains of dead feather pieces from the plumage.

Important: Use fresh water for this, and clean the spraying apparatus regularly.

Claw and Foot Care

At the latest, when a bird can no longer grasp the perch readily or the claws have turned in on themselves, it is necessary to shorten the claws using special fine claw scissors. When you are doing this, you must pay attention to making the cut in the right direction, toward the direction of horny growth, to prevent injury (see drawing).

Important: Don't cut too far down or you will injure the blood vessel and hurt the bird. Hemorrhaging can be life threatening and must be immediately stopped with ferric chloride. If you are unsure about cutting the claws, it's better to go to a veterinarian!

Then the claws are painted with Iodoglycerine to prevent splitting of the horn.

Be careful when trimming claws to cut on the proper slanting angle (see drawing). Don't trim too short!

Every three to four weeks you should paint the toes and legs with Iodoglycerine or Tea Tree Oil. This will help prevent scaly-leg mites (see page 68), hyperkeratosis (see page 87), and bumblefoot ulcers (see page 86).

Important: Never use sandpaper on perches! Use perches of natural wood.

Technique

Vitamins, iodine drops, and glucose are the exception—water to which these have been added is usually drunk gladly.

Administering Medications

Even with the best care and maintenance, a bird can get sick and be prescribed medication.

With the Food

As a general rule, medicines should not be administered via food, because the sick birds often refuse food entirely or ingest only a little. Also, the grains are husked before they are eaten, so any medication adhering to the husk fails to reach its target entirely.

Administering medicine with soft food, however, is possible (see page 115), so long as the birds are still taking in enough food. For this reason, you should get parrots and grain eaters used to soft food ahead of time in order to be able to give them supplementary substances this way.

Some bird fanciers resort to the trick of feeding mealworms with vitamins and minerals or other medications and then offering these "living pills" to the bird as special treats.

With the Drinking Water

Therapy via the drinking water is also problematic. The taste of the water can be so changed by the medication that the bird refuses the water. Some bird species can go without additional water all day long if necessary!

Directly in the Beak

The direct instillation of therapeutic agents into the beak cavity is the most certain means of administration. It should be employed at the first treatment, but you must make sure the patient is in the right position. The body of the bird should be held slanting slightly upward with the head immobilized between the thumb and forefinger.

Fluids should be allowed to run in very slowly with an eye dropper that is placed with its opening at the point of the upper half of the beak.

This method of administration works for birds with straight beaks, as well as for the parrot beak. You can also instill the medication directly into parrots. However, you must use a plastic syringe without a needle. Parrots are sure to bite on the eye droppers and break them if they are glass.

Normally, the patient swallows the medication well. If not, you must immediately abort the attempt and go to a veterinarian!

Ampules

Homeopathic medications in ampules are the best for you to use. They contain no alcohol and are taken without any particular resistance.

Ampules are marked with a dot by the manufacturer. The dot marks where the neck of the ampule is scored at the breaking place. Turn the dot toward you and break the ampule on the opposite side. Then you can easily remove the preparation with an eye dropper and administer it as described above.

Put the eye
dropper at
the point of
the beak and
very carefully
allow a few
drops of the
medication to
trickle in.

In parrots,
the medica-
tion is slowly
dripped into
the beak with
a plastic
syringe
without a
needle.

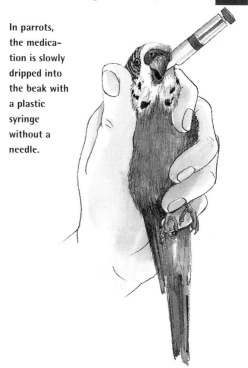

The remainder can be closed up with a piece of tape and stored upright (e.g., in a shot glass), preferably in the refrigerator.

Salves, Tinctures, Sprays

Salves and tinctures are applied with the help of a cotton swab for small areas or a gauze pad or finger for large areas. This way the material can also be spread well.

Spraying the plumage is done at a distance of about 8 in (20 cm). The spray stream should be soft with fine individual drops. If you want to treat a bird for parasites, you must lift all the feathers in order to get the medication through to the skin. The spray material should be warmed slightly beforehand!

Inhalation

Boil an extract (e.g., of chamomile) and put a dish with the hot contents in the cage. The container with its hot contents must, of course, be covered with a sieve or fine-meshed screen to keep the bird from getting into it. Then lay a thick bath towel or a cover over the cage to keep the steam in. Let the patient in-hale the steam for fifteen to thirty minutes daily until the condition being treated im-proves.

Technique

Feeding Sick Birds

Some illnesses require particular diets to support the healing process or to avoid aggravating the condition.

A good supply of minerals and trace elements can be achieved with cuttlefish dishes. They should always be available to your birds. Minerals and trace elements are important, among other things, for the development of bones and tissue.

Force Feeding

This is required if a bird is not taking in food any longer. Because of their high basal metabolic rate, birds very quickly get into an extremely problematic condition with a lack of food.

Make a solution of:
40 ml Catosal
40 ml normal saline solution
5 ml Tricrescovit
2 tsp vitamin C powder
5 tsp dextrose
½ tsp calcium chloride

Give small amounts of this solution drop by drop with an eye dropper at brief intervals. You can also have this mixture prepared by a veterinarian.

Jars of baby food (fruit/fruit salad and spring vegetables), to which you add a supplement of vitamins and minerals, such as Korvimin ZVT, are also suitable for forced feeding of parrots and beos.

Build-up or Breeding Food for Parrots

(from a recipe from the San Diego Zoo)
wheat germ flakes
Gevral protein
pellets for trout (45 percent raw protein content)
shelled sunflower kernels
finely chopped lettuce
corn syrup
fresh egg yolk
vitamin-mineral powder
a little iodized salt
L-cysteine (essential amino acid)
calcium lactate

Tonic

Place
—0.7 oz (20 g) each of calamus root and juniper berries
—0.35 oz (10 g) each of anise and fennel
—rock candy

in 1 qt (1 l) of 96 percent alcohol and let draw for several days.

Then give, as a tonic only, 1 ml (0.03 fl oz) in 50 ml (1.69 fl oz) of drinking water.

Diet for Liver Disease

Basically, the food should be low in protein and fat. Give an abundant amount of fruit and greens and, via the drinking water, supplementary vitamins and amino acids. Also time-tested—especially with ailing parrots—is feeding with jars of baby food (fruit and vegetable preparations).

For a suspected liver disease, give the bird a liver-protecting solution in the drinking water.
Mix
100 ml (3.38 fl oz) glucose
5 ml (0.17 fl oz) Hepsan Syrup

10 ml (0.34 fl oz) multivitamin liquid
15 ml (0.5 fl oz) Plastisan
5 ml (0.17 fl oz) Catosal
and give one ml (0.03 fl oz) in 100 ml (3.38 fl oz) of drinking water.

For direct administration, give one to five drops per day, depending on size.

Kidney-Protecting Solution

For diseases of the urinary system and kidneys (see page 57), a Tyrode's solution is recommended for drinking.

To make it, mix
8.00 g sodium chloride
0.13 g calcium chloride
0.20 g potassium chloride
0.10 g magnesium chloride
0.05 g sodium dihydrogen phosphate
1.00 g sodium bicarbonate
in 1 L of water. In addition, vitamin A and 100 ml glucose should be added.

You can also have the solution prepared by a veterinarian or at a pharmacy.

Gastrointestinal Tea

To prevent gastrointestinal disturbances and gout and stimulate the entire metabolism, the following tea made of dried medicinal plants has proven helpful.
Mix
—10 g (0.35 oz) each of anise, thyme, sage leaves, calendula blossoms, caraway, Saint-John's wort, common milfoil, stinging nettle, and wormwood
—50 g (1.77 oz) blackberry leaves
—30 g (1.06 oz) plantain
—20 g (0.71 oz) stinging nettle root
and let one heaping tablespoon of them draw in 1 qt (1 l) of boiling water for ten to fifteen min-utes. Give the bird the strained, cooled extract once a week instead of drinking water.

Always prepare the tea fresh!

"Light Feed" for Large Parrots

The commercially available feed mixtures of large seeds and grains are often very high in fat and not well balanced.

Try this mixture:
—⅓ carrots, apples, red beets
—⅓ soybeans, green peas, chickpeas, corn
—⅓ pearl barley, sunflower kernels, wheat
Soak the legumes and grains overnight.

In addition, mix in pine nuts and vitamin and mineral mixtures, animal protein, fruit, and greens.

Soft Food

You should offer such feed if your bird cannot eat well, perhaps because of an injury to its beak.

For example, use cottage cheese, hard-boiled egg, egg biscuit or softened zwieback, mixture for soft-food eaters, bananas, cooked rice, and multivitamin supplements.

Diet Tips for Parrots

- To avoid obesity, give large parrots small seeds and an abundance of fruit, greens, and wood to gnaw on.
- To keep them occupied, you can give them small quantities of pine nuts.
- If possible, avoid peanuts with shells. These often contain aspergillus fungus spores.
- Never give your parrot only sunflower seed kernels. They contain too much fat and lead to deficiency conditions.

Index of Home Remedies

On the following pages you will find an overview of all the natural remedies that have been recommended in this book for self-help or prevention and aftercare.

The uses presented refer primarily to the indications (see page 122) discussed here and are not exclusive. The remedies have a broad spectrum of effects.

When the term "Injeel" is appended to the name of the preparation, it refers to a homeopathic single remedy in potency accord, that is, the substance contains single remedies usually in potencies 10X or 12X, 30X, and 200X. "Injeel forte" means that a higher potency (usually 3X, 4X, or 6X) is added to the one named.

All homeopathic single or combination remedies presented here are available in ampules (solutions for injection). These ampules are also suitable as drinking ampules. The solutions can be given directly into the mouth of a bird. The ampules usually have a content of 1.1 or 2.2 ml (cc) and sometimes bear a letter S, N, P, or T after their name. However, these letters have no significance for the average user. In addition there are some medications available in 5 ml ampules for veterinary use. They carry the notation "ad us. vet."

You can get the ampules in homeopathic pharmacies in packages of five, and from a holistic veterinarian (they are also available in single doses). Most of the remedies are also available in tablets or drops. The tablets are especially difficult to give to smaller birds and for some species they are indigestible because they contain lactose; the drops are not suitable for birds because they are mostly preserved in alcohol.

Single and Combination Remedies

Aconitum-Homaccord (Heel)
Active ingredients: Aconite, Eucalyptus, Ipecacuanha in potency accord
Indication: Highly acute infections of the airways, circulatory failure

Aconitum-Injeel (Heel)
Active ingredients: Aconite in potency accord
Indication: Highly acute inflammatory diseases of the airways anxiety, eye inflammations, shock, heat stroke

Argentum nitricum 30X (DHU)
Active ingredients: Argentum nitricum 30X
Indication: Paralyses, coordination problems

Arnica 30X and 200X (DHU)
Arnica-Injeel (Heel)
Active ingredients: Arnica in several potencies
Indications: Brain concussion, shock, injuries (bleeding) from blows or crushing, inflammations

Arsenicum album-Injeel (Heel)
Active ingredients: Acidum arsenicosum in potency accord
Indications: Poisonings, severe exhaustion, inflammations, generalized infections, and gangrene

Belladonna-Homaccord (Heel)
Active ingredients: Belladonna and Echinacea in potency accord
Indications: Localized inflammations, following removal of a foreign body

Berberis-Homaccord (Heel)
Active ingredients: Berberis, Colocynthis, and Veratrum in potency accord
Indications: Inflammations of the urinary tract and liver, diarrhea, gout

Bufo-Injeel (Heel)
Active ingredients: Bufo in potency accord
Indications: Coarse skin vesicles

Cactus compositum (Heel)
Active ingredients: Crataegus 2X, Spigelia 5X, potassium carbonicum 5X, Cactus 3X, Glonoinum 5X
Indication: Heart failure

Calcium fluoratum 12X (DHU)
Active ingredients: Calcium fluoratum 12X
Indications: Stuck in the molt syndrome

Calcium iodatum 12X (DHU)
Active ingredients: Calcium iodatum 12X
Indications: Hypothyroidism, goiter

Calcium phosphoricum-Injeel (Heel)
Active ingredients: Calcium phosphoricum in potency accord
Indications: Gout, rickets

Cantharis compositum (Heel)
Active ingredients: Cantharis 4X, Acidum arsenicosum 8X, Mercurius solubilis Hahnemanni 8X, Hepar sulfuris 8X
Indications: Increases resistance in kidney inflammation

Carbo vegetabilis 200X (DHU)
Carbo vegetabilis-Injeel (Heel)
Active ingredients: Carbo vegetabilis in several potencies
Indications: Shock, heat stroke, circulatory collapse

Carcinoma hepatitis-Injeel (Heel)
Active ingredients: Nosode preparation (see page 122) in potency accord
Indications: Supporting treatment for liver tumors

Carduus compositum (Heel)
(Also under the name of: Hepeel)
Active ingredients: Carduus marianus 1X, Chelidonium 3X, China 2X, Colocynthis 5X, Lycopodium 2X, Nux moschata 3, Veratrum 5X, phosphorus 5X
Indications: Liver function disorder, liver degeneration, metabolic regulation, poisoning, stuck-in-the molt syndrome.

Causticum compositum (Heel)
Active ingredients: Causticum Hahnemanni 3X, Arnica 4X, Pulsatilla 6X, sulfur 12X, and others
Indications: Burns

Cerebrum compositum (Heel)
Active ingredients: Cerebrum suis 8X, Hepar suis 8X, Thuja 6X, ignatia 8X, China 4X, Conium 4X, Aconitum 4X, gelsemium 4X, aesculus 4X, and others
Indications: Brain concussion, diseases of the central nervous system, developmental disorders, feather plucking

Chamomilla-Injeel forte (Heel)
Active ingredients: Chamomilla in potency accord
Indications: Inflammations, painful conditions, egg-binding

Chelidonium-Homaccord (Heel)
Active ingredients: Chelidonium, Belladonna, Fel tauri in potency accord
Indications: Liver damage, gastroenteritis

Coenzyme compositum (Heel)
Active ingredients: Coenzyme A 8X, Pulsatilla 6X, Hepar sulfuris 10X, Sulfur 10X, and many cofactors needed for fermentation, as well as enzymes active in the citric acid cycle.
Indications: To stimulate the metabolism and overall immune resistance

Colchicum-Injeel (Heel)
Active ingredients: Colchicum autumnale in potency accord
Indications: Gout, joint pain, nephritis

Cor compositum (Heel)
Active ingredients: Cor suis 8X, Hepar suis 8X, Arnica 4X, Ignatia 6X, Acidum arsenicosum 8X, g-Strophanthin 8, H_2O 8X, Cactus 3X, Glonoinum 4X, kalmia 4X, and others
Indications: Heart failure, anemia, circulatory problems

Cutis compositum (Heel)
Active ingredients: Cutis suis 8X, Hepar suis 8X, Thuja 8X, Galium 6X, Sulfur 10X, Urtica 4X, Aesculus 6X, Ledum 4X, Pyrogenium 198X, and others
Indications: Skin diseases, horny growths, feather growth disorders

Cuprum aceticum-Injeel (Heel)
Active ingredients: Cuprum aceticum in potency accord
Indications: Cardiovascular insufficiency, tendency to convulsions

Echinacea compostum (Heel)
Active ingredients: Echinacea 3X, Aconitum 3X, Sanguinaria 4X, Sulfur 8X, Baptisia 4X, Lachesis 10X, Bryonia 6X, Pulsatilla 8X, and others
Indications: Stimulation of body's resistance, bacterial infections, air sac inflammation, cold

Engystol (Heel)
Active ingredients: Vincetoxicum, Sulfur in potency accord
Indications: To stimulate immune response in viral disease; general strengthening remedy

Euphorbium compositum (Heel)
Euphorbium compositum Nose Drops (Heel)
Active ingredients: Euphorbium 4X, Pulsatilla 2X, Luffa 6X, Mercurius 8X, Mucosa nasalis suis 8X, Hepar sulfuris 10X, and others
Indications: Colds, sinusitis, respiratory disorders

Galium-Heel (Heel)
Active ingredients: Galium 3X, Sedum acre 3X, Sempervivum 4X, clematis 4X, Thuja 3X, and others
Indications: General enhancement of resistance; chronic diseases, growths, leukosis associated changes (see page 122)

Gelsemium 30X (DHU)
Active ingredients: Gelsemium 30X
Indications: Shock, paralysis, convulsions

Gelsemium-Homaccord (Heel)
Active ingredients: Gelsemium, Rhus toxicodendron, Cimicifuga in potency accord
Indications: Stimulation of resistance to poisons, tumors

Graphites-Homaccord (Heel)
Active ingredients: Graphites, Calcium carbonicum in potency accord
Indications: Chronic dry eczema, keratin scales, brittle beak, horny growths, beak and claw deformities

Hepar compositum (Heel)
Active ingredients: Hepar suis 8X, China 4X, Lycopodium 4X, Chelidonium 4X, Carduus 3X, Fel tauri 8X, Sulfur 13X, and others
Indications: Liver diseases, metabolic disorders, skin diseases

Hepar sulfuris-Injeel (Heel)

Active ingredients: Hepar sulfuris in potency accord
Indications: Suppuration, bumble foot

Hormeel (Heel)

Active ingredients: Senecio 6X, Acidum nitricum 4X, Moschus 6X, Pulsatilla 4X, Sepia 6X, Ignatia 6X, and others
Indications: Fertility disorders, hormonal molting disorders, hormonal beak growth, tumors, continued egg laying

Ignatia 30X and 200X (DHU) Ignatia-Injeel (Heel)

Active ingredients: Strychnos ignatii in several potencies
Indications: Nervousness, separation shock, paralyses

Lachesis compositum ad us. vet. (Heel)

Active ingredients: Lachesis 6X, Pyrogenium 6X, Echinacea 1X, Pulsatilla 2X, Sabina 3X
Indications: Oviduct inflammation, peritonitis, infected wounds

Ledum-Injeel (Heel)

Active ingredients: Ledum palustre in potency accord
Indications: Gout, bumble foot

Lycopodium-Injeel (heel)

Active ingredients: Lycopodium in potency accord
Indications: Pancreatic disorders, liver damage

Lymphomyosot (Heel)

Active ingredients: Myosotis arvensis 3X, Veronica 3X, Teucrium 3X, Pinus 4X, Juglans 3X, and others
Indications: Tumors, leukosis (see page 122), xanthomatoses

Mucosa compositum (Heel)

Active ingredients: Mucosa suis 8X, Argentum nitricum 6X, Belladonna 10X, Phosphorus 8X, Anacardium 6X, Veratrum 4X, Pulsatilla 6X, and others
Indications; Mucosal diseases, air sac inflammation, crop inflammation, egg-binding

Mucosa nasalis suis-Injeel (Heel)

Active ingredients: Mucosa nasalis suis in potency accord
Indications: Colds, sinusitis

Naphthalin-Injeel (Heel)

Active ingredients: Naphthalinum in potency accord
Indications: Chronic lower respiratory disease

Natrium Homaccord (Heel)

(In US-made preparations: Sodium Homaccord)
Active ingredients: Sodium carbonicum, Sodium chloratum, Sodium nitricum in potency accord
Indications: Chronic disorders of the mucosal surfaces and of the skin, brittle beak, beak mites

Natrium muriaticum 6X (DHU)

Active ingredients: Sodium chloratum 6X
Indications: Stuck-in-the-molt syndrome

Nux vomica-Homaccord (Heel)

Active ingredients: Nux vomica, Bryonia, Lycopodium, Colocynthis in potency accord
Indications: Digestive disorders, crop inflammations, diarrhea, constipation, diet induced disorders, paralyses, poisoning

Ovarium compositum (Heel)

Active ingredients: Ovarium suis 8X, Lilium tigrinum 4X, Pulsatilla 18X, Sepia 10X, Creosotum 8X, Bovista 6X, Hydrastis 4X, and others
Indications: Oviduct inflammation, oviduct prolapse, hormonal molting disorders, failure to lay or hatch, ovarian tumors

Paeonia officinalis-Injeel forte (Heel)

Active ingredients: Paeonia officinalis in potency accord
Indications: Inflammations of the cloaca and the uropygeal gland

Populus compositum (Heel)

Active ingredients: Populus, Sabal, Capsicum 3X, Bucco 3X, Camphora 3X, Apis 3X, Solidago 3X, Petroselinum 3X, Baptisia 3X, Scilla 3X, Berberis 5X, Cantharis 5X, and others
Indications: Kidney diseases, gout

Psorinoheel (Heel)

Active ingredients: Psorinum 10X, Medorrhinum 12X, Sulfur 6X, Thuja 6X, Bufo 10X, Luesinum 12X, Natrium chloratum 12X, and others
Indications: General conditioning remedy for skin disorders, brittle beak, beak mites

Pulmonaria vulgaris-Injeel (Heel)

Active ingredients: Pulmonaria officinalis in potency accord
Indications: Lower respiratory disease

Pulsatilla compositum (Heel)

Active ingredients: Pulsatilla 6X, Sulfur 8X, and others
Indications: General disorders, malformed eggs

Pulsatilla 4X (DHU)

Active ingredients: Pulsatilla pratensis 4X
Indications: Egg-binding

Restructa forte ST (Fides)
Active ingredients: Colchicum 4X, Berberis 2X, Bryonia 4X, formica rufa, Lithium Chloratum 3X, rhus toxicodendron 4X, silicea 6X, and others
Indications: Gout, arthritic changes, kidney insufficiency
Available as: only as tablets (quantities of 70 and 250)

Rhus Tox-Injeel (Heel)
Active ingredients: Rhus toxicodendron in potency accord
Indications: Joint inflammations, paralysis

Silicea 12X (DHU)
Active ingredients: Acidum silicium 12X
Indications: Stuck-in-the-molt syndrome

Solidago compositum (Heel)
Active ingredients: Solidago 3X, Berberis 4X, Terebinthina 6X, Baptisia 4X, Cantharis 6X, and others
Indications: Kidney diseases

Sulfur 200X (Heel/DHU)
Active ingredients: Sulfur 200X
Indications: Chronic diseases, collapse

Sulfur-Injeel forte (Heel)
Active ingredients: Sulfur in potency accord
Indications: Skin diseases, fungal infections, otitis, ear inflammations, xanthematosis, conditioning remedy

Testis compositum (Heel)
Active ingredients: Testis suis 4X Ginseng 4X, Damiana 8X, Agnus castus 6X, and others
Indications: Male fertility problems

Tea Tree oil
Active ingredients: Melaleuca alternifolia
Indications: Skin problems, fungal infections, hyperberatosis
Available as: Tea tree essence

Thuja-Injeel (Heel)
Active ingredients: Thuja occidentalis in potency accord
Indications: Warts

Thyreoidea compositum (Heel)
Active ingredients: Thyreoidea suis 8X, Galium 4X, Splen suis 10X, Sedum 6X, Conium 4X, spongia 8X, Colchicum 4X, Viscum album 3X, and others
Indications: Thyroid disorders, fatty liver degeneration, tumors

Traumeel (Heel)
Active ingredients: Arnica 2X, Calendula 2X, Hamamelis 2X, Millefolium 3X, Belladonna 4X, Aconitum 3X, Mercurius 8X, Hepar sulfuris 8X, Chamomilla 3X, Symphytum 8X, Bellis perennis 2X, Echinacea 2X
Indications: Wounds, bruises, burns, abscesses, sprains, fractures, concussions, shock, otitis, arthritis
Available as: ampules four at 2.2 ml, five at 5 ml), ointment for external use (50 g and 100 g)

Ubichinon compositum (Heel)
Active ingredients: Coenzyme Q_{10}, Myrtillus 4X, Colchicum 4X, Podophyllum 4X, Conium 4X, Hydrastis 4X, Sulfur 8X, Para-benzochinon 10X, and others
Indications: Degenereative diseases, tumors, resistance to poisons

Veratrum-Homaccord (Heel)
Active ingredients: Veratrum, Aloe, Tormentilla, Rheum in potency accord
Indications: Diarrhea, crop inflammation, circulatory disease

Zeel (Heel)
Active ingredients: Cartilago suis, Rhus toxicodendron, Arnica, Dulcamara, Symphytum, and others
Indications: Joint inflammations, sprains, fractures
Available as: ampules ten at 2.2 ml, five at 5 ml), ointment for external use (50 g and 100 g)

Bach Flowers

The 38 Bach Flowers are widely sold in homeopathic pharmacies in all holistic veterinary clinics, and in most healthfood stores. They are sold in 10 ml stock bottles that contain the essences from which dilutions are made. Rescue Remedy essence is also sold in 20 cc bottles and in the form Rescue Remedy cream.

The individual flowers are:

Agrimony
Aspen
Beech
Centaury
Cerato
Cherry Plum
Chestnut Bud
Chicory
Clematis
Crab Apple
Elm
Gentian
Gorse
Heather
Holly
Honeysuckle
Hornbeam
Impatiens
Larch
Mimulus
Oak
Olive
Pine
Red Chestnut
Rock Rose
Rock Water
Scleranthus
Star of Bethlehem

Sweet Chestnut
Vervain
Vine
Walnut
Water Violet
White Chestnut
Wild Oat
Wild Rose
Willow

In addition to the single Bach Flower essences there is the Rescue Remedy essence that consists of a combination of Cherry Plum, Clematis, Impatiens, Rock Rose, Star of Bethlehem.

Other Recommended Remedies

Arnica Tincture (Plantavet)
Active ingredients: Tinctura Arnicae
Indications: Blunt injuries like crushing, sprains, bruises, otitis
Available as: bottles of 100 ml

Catosal (Bayer)
Active ingredients: Butafosfan, Cyanocobalamin, methyl-4-hydroxybenzoate, phosphorus
Indications: Metabolic disorders, developmental and dietary disorders in young animals; for overexertion and exhaustion

Available as: bottles of 100 ml

Exner Petguard (Exner)
Active ingredients: Water, oil, whey protein, sugar monohydrate, ash
Indications: Ecological insecticide, skin and feather care
Available as: bottles of 100 ml and 1000 ml; spray bottles of 100 ml and 500 ml.

Hepsan-Sirup (Minden)
Active ingredients: N-acetyl-DL-menthionine, choline salt, riboflavin, nicotinamide, cyanocobalamin
Indications: Chronic and subacute, liver disorders like fatty liver and cirrhosis of the liver; protects the liver
Available as: bottles of 100 g

Korvimin ZVT (WDT)
Active ingredients: Dicalcium phosphate, calcium carbonate, powdered whey, yeast, sodium chloride, vitamins A, D_3, E, C, B_1, B_2, B_6, B_{12}, calcium-D-pantothenate, nicotinic acid, folic acid, biotin, vitamin K_3, iron, manganese, zinc, copper, cobalt, iodine, molybdenum, selenium, and amino acids
Indications: Augmentation of diet; symptoms of vitamin, mineral, and trace element deficiencies, molting; stress conditions, growth; reproduction

Available as: packages of 200 g and 1 kg (one and two pounds)

Cod-liver oil–Zinc
Ointment (Alvetra)
Active ingredients: cod-liver oil, zinc oxide
Indications: For treatment of eczema, poorly healing wounds, burns
Available as: Ointment

Plastisan (Alvetra)
Active ingredients: Iron (III) glycerophosphate, glycerinophosphoric acid- calcium, -magnesium, sodium, methanearsonic acid, disodium, manganese (II) chloride
Indications: Deficiency diseases, anemia
Available as: bottles of 100, 250, 500, and 1000 ml

Ticrescovit (Rhone Merieux)
Active ingredients: Vitamins A, B, B_1, B_2, B_6, B_{12}, pantothenic acid-sodium, nicotinamide, cholecalciferol-cholesterin, vitamin E acetate, liver extract.
Indications: Multivitamin preparation; vitamin B deficiency, metabolic disorders; liver disorders during molting
Available as: bottles of 50 and 100 ml

Glossary

Aerosol vaccine
Vaccine that is administered through inhalation.

Allopathy
Hahnemann's term for the classic form of (western) medical treatment, as opposed to homeopathy.

Avian influenza
Another name for Newcastle disease, see page 122.

Blood feather
Newly emerging immature feather containing blood vessels.

Bristle feathers
These small specialized feathers surround the base of the beak of the bird and also form the eyelashes. These feathers are not barbed, are very fine, and are equipped with many sensory cells that allow the birds a variety of sensory perceptions.

Cardiac insufficiency
Weak heart; inability of the heart muscle to keep the rate of blood flow high enough.

Carrier
A carrier of pathogens continues to shed agents that cause disease in other species but not in the carrier.

Chlamydia
Cocci-shaped bacteria that infect warm-blooded animals. They cause the disease Ornithosis (see page 122), and therefore the disease is also called "Chlamydiosis."

Cloaca
Combined anal orifice for the excretion of feces, urine, and reproductive fluids.

Clostridium
A rod-shaped, anaerobic bacterium that produces gases.

Coccidia
Intestinal parasites (protozoans); among other diseases, they cause particular harm to canaries in the form of a hemorrhatic intestinal disease. Can occur in all birds. Spreads by the massive shedding of oocytes. Animals with lowered resistance are especially at risk.

Constitution
Physical, emotional, and spiritual condition; level of susceptibility to disease.

Contour feathers
They form the entire outer plumage and protect the bird from water. Contour feathers as divided in flight- or wing-feathers and tail feathers.

Down
The first feathers of the chick. The vanes of the down are not bound to the radii [small barbules] with hooklets (see inside front cover).

Dyspnea
Difficult or labored respiration.

Ectoparasites
Parasites of the skin and/or the feathers.

Eczema
Dry or moist inflammation of the skin

Endoparasite
Parasites of the internal organs, e.g., worms.

Endoscopy
Examination of the internal organs with a special optical device that can be introduced to the interior of the body through a small incision.

Feather follicle
The seat of the feather in the skin.

Filoplume
Feathers with a long, fine shaft that are located next to the contour feathers (see page 121). Their feather follicle is equipped with many fine nerve endings. Possibly, the filoplumes function like a kind of antenna that provides for the optimal alignment of the contour feathers.

First worsening
The initial reaction of the body to homeopathic treatment with single remedies may be an aggravation of disease symptoms.

Fowl diphtheria
See Pox.

Grit
Small, fine stone particles, important for the digestive system of the grain eaters as "substitute teeth."

Homotoxicology
Theory according to which diseases are the expression of defense mechanisms against internal and external toxins. Was proposed by the physician Dr. Hans-Heinrich Reckeweg in 1952 (see page 26).

Indication
List of symptoms or diseases that form the basis for use of a particular therapy and a certain medication.

Keratin
Protein of horny material of the beak, feathers, cere, and nails.

Leukosis
Viral disease of the white blood cells, affecting the immune system.

Leukotic changes
Enlarged lymphoid organs

Magnetic-field therapy
Therapy with electromagnetic waves.

Melanismus
Dark coloration of the skin and/or the feathers produced by the pigment cells (melanocytes).

Neurosis
Emotional disturbance that expresses itself in behavior that deviates from the norm, e.g., overwhelming anxiety, depression, hysteria, or compulsive repetition.

Newcastle disease
Infectious disease of the eyes and airway in birds; is caused by paramyxovirus (see inside back cover).

Nosode
Use of organic and metabolic noninfectious products for medicinal preparations. The effect of nosodes is the detoxification of the body. A "broad-spectrum" nosode is Psorinoheel.

Oral
Administration via the beak.

Ornithosis
Infectious disease, caused by *Chlamydia*, that produces disease primarily of the eyes and airway in birds. Earlier it was known as psittacosis (parrot fever), because parrots were primarily responsible for the transmission of the disease to humans. This is a reportable disease.

Osteomalacia
Bone softness and a tendency to bend as a result of inadequate incorporation of minerals.

Parasite
An organism that lives in or on another organism and uses the host for its own advantage.

Paratyphus
See Salmonelloses.

Parrot fever
See Ornithosis.

PBFD
Psittacine beak and feather disease, also known as beak necrosis or feather-loss syndrome. This viral disease is characterized by immune deficiency and usually ends in death.

per os
Latin for "by mouth," referring to administration of medication by means of the beak and the digestive system.

Polyuria
Pathological (abnormal) increase in the amount of urine.

Potency accord
A homeopathic single remedy prepared in specific potencies.

Powder feathers
They scatter tiny keratin particles as a fine white powder, which probably helps make the contour feathers waterproof. The powder feathers occur as down, semidown, and contour feathers.

Pox
Disease caused by various fowl pox viruses that (in the cutaneous form) is visible as raised lesions of the skin (pox). The course of the disease may be acute or chronic. In the acute form, there is severe dyspnea. The canary pox virus is the best known.

Psittacosis
See Ornithosis.

Quarantine
Removal of animals to a room separate from their cagemates for a specific period of time in order to lessen the risk of spreading disease.

Salmonelloses
Diseases that are triggered by *Salmonella* (gram-negative bacteria), such as euteritis.

Semi down
This feathering lies under the contour feathers. Its task is principally to insulate warmth, therefore the vane is fluffy-soft.

Simillimum
Similar. Homeopathic medication; in a healthy person, this type of remedy would cause the same symptoms as those against which it is used in a sick person. The name comes from the therapeutic principle of homeopathy: like is treated with like.

Wind eggs
Thin-shelled or shell-less partially desiccated eggs, which are caused by a malfunction in calcium deposit or by calcium deficiency of the hen.

Syrinx
Lower part of the larynx at the point where the trachea branches off; organ of voice formation in birds.

Trauma
Injury, wound, effect of force.

Trichomonads
Flagellated one-celled animals.

Ulcer
Open inflammation of all layers of the skin with a poor tendency to heal.

Urate
End product of nitrogen metabolism.

Uric acid
End product of nitrogen metabolism, formed in the liver and excreted by birds together with the feces as creamy-white urate.

Xanthoma
Disease of the skin with thick, yellow nodules

Zoonosis
Disease that is transmissible from animals to humans (see inside back cover).

Index

Useful Literature

Bach, Edward, *Heal Thyself.* The CW Daniel Comp. Ltd.,1931.

Deiser, Rudolf, *Natural Health Care for Your Cat.* Barron's Educational Series, Inc., Hauppauge, New York 1997.

Rose, Barry, *The Family Health Guide to Homeopathy.* Celestial Arts, Berkeley, California, 1995.

Stein, Petra, *Natural Health Care for Your Dog.* Barron's Educational Series, Inc., Hauppauge, New York, 1997.

Vithoulkas, George, *The Science of Homeopathy.* Random House, Inc., New York, 1980.

Useful Addresses

American Holistic Veterinarian
Medical Association
2214 Old Emmorton Road
Bel Air, MD 21015
(410) 569-0795 (nationwide referrals)

International Foundation for Homeopathy
2366 Eastlake Avenue E.
Suite 301
Seattle, WA 98102
(206) 324-8230

National Center for Homeopathy
801 North Fairfax Street, Suite 306
Alexandria, VA 22314
(703) 548-7790

Nelson Bach, USA, Ltd.
Wilmington Technology Park
100 Research Drive
Wilmington, MA 01887-4406
(800) 334-0843

VIP
Pet Health Insurance
4175 E. La Palma Ave., Suite 100
Anaheim, CA 02807

For Purchase of Remedies Mentioned in This Book

Most of the remedies listed in this book are available in homeopathic pharmacies. Bach Flower essences and a basic supply of homeopathic and herbal remedies are also found in most modern health food stores. If you live in an area where no suitable stores are available you can purchase most of the remedies by mail order.

Photographers

Anders: pages C1, 4 left, 11, 12, 13 left, 16, C4;
Angermayer: pages 2–3, 30–31;
Bilder Pur/Lenz: pages 19 left;
Bilder Pur/Reinhard: pages 1, 5, 24–25;
Bilder Pur/Steimer: page 19 right;
Juniors/Liebold: pages 102–103;
Juniors/Wegler: pages 4 right, 10;
Martin: pages 23;
Morgan/Reinhard: pages 6–7;
Reinhard: pages 8, 9, 13 right, 15 left, 17, 18, 20, 21, 27;
Rittrich-Dorenkamp: page 29;
Wegler: page 15 right.

The Author

Dr. Bernhard Dorenkamp is a practicing veterinarian with an additional specialty in homeopathic medicine. After studying Agricultural Science in Osnabrück and veterinary medicine in Hannover, he wrote a doctoral thesis on the subject of "coccidiosis in the goose." Since 1983 he has worked in his own veterinary clinic in East Westphalia and has continued to foster a special interest in avian medicine.

He has acquired extensive knowledge in homeopathic medicine. He has also, as a member of the Academy for Veterinary Sciences—held countless seminars on the subject of biomedical sciences in the field of veterinary medicine. Furthermore, he has published an impressive number of scientific papers. Recently his clinic has been awarded accreditation as an institute for advanced training in veterinary application and study of homeopathy.

Imprint

Published originally under the title *Naturheilpraxis Vögel* © 1997 by Gräfe und Unzer Verlag GmbH, München

English translation © Copyright 1998 by Barron's Educational Series, Inc.

All inquiries should be addressed to:
Barron's Educational Series, Inc.
250 Wireless Boulevard
Hauppauge, New York 11788
http://www.barronseduc.com

Library of Congress Catalog Card No.
98-72210

International Standard Book Number
0-7641-0124-2

Printed in Hong Kong

9 8 7 6 5 4 3 2 1